SUMMA PUBLICATIONS, INC.

Thomas M. Hines
Publisher

Norris J. Lacy
Editor-in-Chief

Editorial Board

Benjamin F. Bart
University of Pittsburgh

William Berg
University of Wisconsin

Germaine Brée
Wake Forest University

Michael Cartwright
McGill University

Hugh M. Davidson
University of Virginia

John D. Erickson
Louisiana State University

Wallace Fowlie
Duke University (Emeritus)

James Hamilton
University of Cincinnati

Freeman G. Henry
University of South Carolina

Edouard Morot-Sir
*University of North Carolina
Chapel Hill*

Jerry C. Nash
University of New Orleans

Albert Sonnenfeld
Princeton University

Ronald W. Tobin
*University of California
Santa Barbara*

Philip A. Wadsworth
University of South Carolina (Emeritus)

ORDERS:
  Box 20725
  Birmingham, AL 35216

EDITORIAL ADDRESS:
  1904 Countryside
  Lawrence, KS 66044

The Journey of Charlemagne to Jerusalem and Constantinople

(Le Voyage de Charlemagne à Jérusalem et à Constantinople)

The Journey of Charlemagne to Jerusalem and Constantinople

(Le Voyage de Charlemagne à Jérusalem et à Constantinople)

edited and translated

by

Jean-Louis G. Picherit

Summa Publications, Inc.
Birmingham, Alabama

Copyright 1984
Summa Publications, Inc.
ISBN 0-917786-08-4
Library of Congress Catalog Number 84-52505
Printed in the United States of America

TO RITA

CONTENTS

Introduction i

Text and Translation 1

Notes 76

Index of Proper Names 84

Select Bibliography 88

Foreword

This is the first complete English translation of the *Voyage* (or *Pèlerinage*) *de Charlemagne à Jérusalem et à Constantinople.* It is based on our new critical edition (published facing the English text) and is designed primarily for advanced undergraduate and graduate students. It was felt that this short and entertaining poem could be used in conjunction with the austere masterpiece of medieval French literature, the *Chanson de Roland*.

Introduction

Medieval epic poems are among the earliest surviving literary works in Old French. They began to appear at the very end of the eleventh century, with probably the *Chanson de Roland* as their oldest example. These poems, called "chansons de geste" in French, express the values and reflect the structure of eleventh and twelfth-century society which was based upon Christianity and feudalism. Most of these works recount the high deeds of Christian heroes who have sworn allegiance to a Carolingian king. This suzerain, who usually is Charlemagne, leads the Franks and their allies against the pagan Saracens. Generally, these epics have a tenuous historical basis, but most of the events and characters are fictitious (although they are presented as entirely true and real by the jongleurs who recite them). The first poems, such as the *Roland*, do not include more than a few thousand verses, usually of ten syllables. These lines are often assonanced, which means that their last words have an identical vowel sound followed by a different final consonant. Verses with the same assonance form a strophe called *laisse*, which can be of any length. The *chansons de geste* were presented—and sometimes written down—by jongleurs who were itinerant public entertainers. These performers often used a musical instrument, like a *vielle* or a *rote*, to accompany their chanting of the poems before the noble audience of a castle or before the crowds of the marketplace.

Cycle Classification of Epics

Many epics of the twelfth and thirteenth centuries celebrate the deeds of the same families of heroes. For this reason, Bertrand de Bar-sur-Aube classified these poems into three main groups, or cycles. In the *Geste du roi*, or cycle of the King, the King of France, usually Charlemagne, plays an important role. He is depicted as a powerful and majestic figure leading his men in battle against the Saracens—as for example in the *Chanson de Roland* and the *Chanson d'Aspremont*—and bringing victory to Christendom. A second group of epics deals with the adventures of the King as he takes action against a rebel subject. These poems are often referred to as the rebellious vassal cycle, or the *Geste de Doon de Mayence*, named after a notorious vassal of Charlemagne. In contrast to his portrayal in the King cycle as the majestic leader of the West, Charlemagne in this group of epics often appears as a mean, unforgiving suzerain, unrelenting in his pursuit of a vassal who has caused him some harm (e.g., *Renaud de Montauban* or *Girard de Roussillon*). The third cycle includes twenty-four epics relating the adventures of William of Orange, his father, Aymeri, and his ancestors. It is commonly called after William, the hero of the oldest poem, the *Chanson de Guillaume*.

However, not all *chansons de geste* fit into one of these three cycles. Some of them were inspired by contemporary history, as is the case with the *Chanson d'Antioche* and the *Chanson de Jérusalem* which were based on the First Crusade. The *Chétifs*, the *Enfances Godefroy*, and the *Chevalier au cygne* also reflect the same historical event, but they are more fictional. Modern critics have often referred to these poems as the "Crusade cycle." Another example of a minor group is the "Relic cycle," alluded to in the *Mort Aymeri de Narbonne*. Most of the works belonging to this family of poems are now lost.

Evolution and Continued Popularity of the "Chansons de geste"

Toward the end of the twelfth century, the epic was influenced by a new medieval genre, the romance. Love and various folk themes began to permeate the *chansons de geste* to such an extent that they were completely transformed. Today, many of these works of the thirteenth and fourteenth centuries are called, more appropriately, *chansons d'aventures*. Some of these, especially the last representatives of the waning genre, reached mammoth proportions; *Lion de Bourges*, for example, numbers some 34,298 verses. However, the stories survived until the nineteenth century in long prose versions. Some of them, like *Fierabras* and *Huon de Bordeaux*, appeared as chapbooks and in the *Bibliothèque Bleue*, a popular collection, which ceased publication in 1863. The considerable success of this medieval genre is further illustrated by numerous translations and adaptations in various languages, both during and after the Middle Ages. Noteworthy among these are the *Karlamagnus saga*, a Norse compilation of Old French epics dealing with Charlemagne, prepared around 1300 for the King of Norway, and an Italian collection put together by Andrea de Barberino at the end of the Middle Ages under the title *Reali di Francia*.

The "Voyage de Charlemagne"

Although the *Chanson de Roland* and the *Voyage de Charlemagne* are usually included in the same *Geste du roi*, no two poems could be more dissimilar. The *Voyage* is very short (870 lines), about one quarter of the length of the *Roland* (4002 lines), and it is written in twelve-syllable verses, rather than the usual ten-syllable lines. While the *Roland* has a historical base—i.e. Charlemagne's expedition into Spain and the destruction of his rear guard in the Pyrenees on August 15, 778—the account of the Emperor's journey to Jerusalem and Constantinople is entirely based on legend. The ruler of the Franks never intervened militarily in the Middle East or even travelled there. While the historical event at the heart of the *Roland* permitted nineteenth-century critics (for example, G. Paris in his *Histoire poètique de Charlemagne*, 1865) to theorize that medieval epics originated on battlefields in Charlemagne's day, when soldiers and jongleurs started to sing lyric poems relating these events, the ahistorical *Voyage* gave J. Bédier (*Les Légendes épiques*, 1908-1913) a solid argument in support of a different theory. He believed that the *chansons de geste* were based on legends developed by monks, long after the historical events in question.

Tone and Atmosphere of the Poem

But it is above all by its tone and atmosphere that the *Voyage* distinguishes itself from the *Roland*. On the one hand, we have a light and jocular poem narrating the comical adventures of Charlemagne; on the other, we are presented with a superb but violent epic depicting the struggle between Good and Evil. In spite of a lack of agreement among scholars on the specific intent of the poet, many would agree that the *Voyage* is a comical work based on the heroic literary tradition. What predominates in this poem is the author's hearty good humor, exemplified by the Queen's comments in the opening scene (13-16, 26-29, 32-38), by the reactions of the Jew in Jerusalem (129-140), and by the episode of the boasts (453-617). In these scenes, the poet uses a bantering tone as, for example, when the Queen interrupts a very solemn ceremony, and when the Jew asks to be baptized after mistaking Charlemagne for God. The poet is entertaining his audience; he is not trying to ridicule or to satirize the Emperor or his French vassals, contrary to what H. J. Neuschäfer (1959, pp. 83, 96-97) and T. Heinermann (1936) have stated. The cleverness of the poet shows up again when he is describing Hugo's majestic palace and his immense wealth (342-363). Charlemagne is so impressed by what he discovers that he feels humbled and cannot help remembering the Queen's vexing talk about Hugo's preeminence (364). Perhaps she was right, after all. The author again puts the proud Frenchmen to the test in the episode of Hugo's rotating palace (385-391). Although the Frenchmen are badly treated and Charlemagne is sitting on the floor (387), he still maintains his dignity. The Belgian scholar J. Horrent (1961, p. 64) has pointed out that the episode of the boasts shows that the poet is not treating his subject seriously and is concerned primarily with entertaining his audience, for "the laughter raised by the scene of the boasts does not turn against the Frenchmen, does not ridicule them, . . . the comical impression is not created at their expense: the poet wants people to laugh with them, not at them" (p. 75).

Relics play a major part in the *Voyage* and contribute to its unity. Their detailed description (160-203, 255-258) has sometimes been judged irreverent and ridiculous (T. Heinermann, 1936, p. 523; P. Aebischer, 1956, p. 163; H. J. Neuschäfer, 1959, p. 89; G. Favati, 1965, p. 54), but as J. Horrent has shown (1961, pp. 39-45), all were considered authentic by the audience of the time and were venerated in a number of shrines. But, if they are not ridiculed by the poet when they are handed over by the Patriarch, their display during the performance of the boasts adds to the humor. Although it is God who intervenes to help the French, it is difficult to forget the miracles that the relics have accomplished in Jerusalem and on the road to Constantinople (192-195, 255-258). After keeping his audience in suspense, the poet forgets about the relics and implicates God Himself. Were the relics not quite powerful enough in these circumstances? Was the performance of the boasts too risqué? At any rate it is rather unexpected that the author would substitute God for the relics, at the last moment, when everyone was awaiting them. This is another example of the good-natured and joking attitude of the poet toward an important and serious subject.

This humor of the author of the *Voyage*—characterized by some critics as truly Parisian—seems free of any parodic or caricatural intent, because in the work there is no deliberate attempt at distortion or mockery. In the well-known *chantefable* of *Aucassin et Nicolette*, many elements of the epic are parodied. For example, when the young Aucassin finally decides to fight with his father, Garin de Beaucaire, his actions are burlesque (Roques, pp. 10-12) and, in the land of Torelore, the knights battle using rotten apples, eggs and cheese (p. 31). The poet of the *Voyage* was familiar with the French epic tradition and used it fancifully. Frenchmen go to the Middle East unarmed and mounted on mules, and Charlemagne defeats Hugo without waging war, without fighting even a single pitched battle. This is not in itself a parody of epic themes, as seen by some critics (for example, H. J. Neuschäfer, 1959; G. Favati, 1965, p. 79). But, as Walpole (1963) commented, "What he (the poet) has done . . . is not to degrade or ridicule the emblems of these (Christian) beliefs, Charlemagne, the Queen, the Patriarch, the Jew, the peers, the relics, Hugh, or Hugh's daughter, but to secularize them" (p. 143).

Sources of the Poem

This rapid assessment of the special atmosphere of the poem may help illuminate the circumstances that led a medieval poet to write this unique work. We do not believe that this fanciful composition, based on the translation of the relics of the Passion from the Middle East to the French Abbey of Saint-Denis was written gratuitously. This question in particular has been debated by scholars, because it relates directly to the difficult task of dating the work. Unfortunately the results have been inconclusive. Using internal evidence, some critics (for example, P. Paris, 1859) have argued that the peaceful journey to the Middle East was an accurate reflection of the political climate a few years before the First Crusade. Others, like F. Schürr (1926) and T. Heinermann (1936), saw in the work a satire of the Second Crusade led by Louis VII. Thus the date of composition ascribed to the *Voyage* has depended upon the relation, often tenuous and artificial, established between a few minor allusions and historical events, and has varied from the second half of the eleventh (P. Paris, 1859; G. Paris, 1880 . . .) to the thirteenth century (L. Moland, 1866). In *Les Légendes épiques* (vol. IV, pp. 122-156) J. Bédier stressed the importance of the translation of the relics. Among the few clerical works recounting the legend of Charlemagne's journey to the Orient is a chronicle written about the year 1000 by an Italian Benedictine monk, Benedetto de San Andrea del Soratte, based on chapter XVI of the *Vita Karoli* by Eginhard. Eginhard affirmed that diplomatic relations had been established between Charlemagne and Aaron (Harun al-Rashid), the King of the Persians; Benedetto claimed that the Emperor himself had journeyed to the Middle East to bring back relics for the monastery of San Andrea. A second, slightly later chronicle that figured prominently in Bédier's discussion was the *Descriptio qualiter Karolus Magnus clavum et coronam Domini a Constantinopoli Aquisgrani detulerit qualiterque Karolus Calvus hec ad Sanctum Dyonisium retulerit*. This short text described the relics of the Passion in the Treasury of Saint-Denis and recounted how they got there. Charlemagne went to Constantinople to rescue the Emperor Constantine and the Patriarch of Jerusalem who were besieged by the Saracens. In Constantine's capital, he was offered many worldly gifts, but he refused them, asking instead for some of the relics of the Passion. He was given: eight thorns from the Crown of Thorns, one of the nails of the Cross, the Holy Shroud, the Virgin's shift, one of Simeon's arms, the swaddling clothes of the Child Jesus, and a fragment of the True Cross. Miracles came to be associated with these relics and, at Aix-la-Chapelle, Charlemagne established an annual feast, during the second week of June, for the veneration of these relics. After the death of Charlemagne, Charles the Bald removed some of the relics from the cathedral of Aix: the Holy Shroud went to Saint-Cornelius of Compiègne, and a nail of the Cross, the Crown of Thorns, a fragment of the Cross, and other items went to the Abbey of Saint-Denis. At Saint-Denis, an important religious celebration honoring the relics was held, during the Summer ember-days, in conjunction with a fair called the *Lendit*.

The author of the *Voyage* was probably familiar with the *Descriptio*, for his work contains references to it. Bédier determined that the *Descriptio* was composed shortly after 1109, the year when the Bishop of Paris started to venerate a fragment of the True Cross, a relic that he had received the year before. The Bishop's public celebration took place in his domain, near Saint-Denis, during the Summer ember-days. In Bédier's opinion, the monks of the Abbey wanted to share in the benefits and prestige associated with the Bishop's fair, the *Lendit*. For this reason, they produced relics that they could exhibit at the same time, and the *Descriptio* to justify them. Bédier concluded that the *Voyage* was written after 1109.

Circumstances and Background of the Composition

Other scholars, among them G. Paris (1880), have dated the *Descriptio* before 1095, basing their finding on the statement in the Latin work that the Summer ember-days were still observed during the second week in June. (The date of this religious celebration was moved to Whitsuntide by Pope Urban II in 1095.) Bédier argued that, since the *Descriptio* was basically a false document, its author used the former date of the celebration to make it look archaic and authentic. However, L. Levillain (1927) has convincingly shown that Saint-Denis had its own relics of the Passion by June 10, 1047; that the first *Lendit*, sponsored by the monks, was held as early as June 8, 1048; and that the *Descriptio* was written about 1080. Levillain also pointed out the existence of another *Lendit*, created by Louis VI probably between 1110 and 1112, that was held in the Plaine-Saint-Denis, close to Saint-Denis, at the same time as the original one. It is at this royal *Lendit* that the Bishop of Paris would come in procession to give his blessing with the fragment of the True Cross. The monks of Saint-Denis agitated to control this fair and, in 1124, the King relinquished this right to them. The competition of the King's *Lendit* was certainly more vexing because of the Bishop's celebration of his relic, another fragment of the Cross. It was a clear challenge to Saint-Denis which claimed to have most of the relics of the Passion, *including* a fragment of the Cross. The prestige involved in these two rival celebrations must have strained considerably the relations between both parties. Each side was probably vying with the other, claiming to have the "authentic" relic of the Cross, and endeavoring to justify it to the crowds which attended the *Lendits*. It is quite likely that the *Descriptio* was used again by the monks in their dispute. The author of the *Voyage* was doubtless inspired by just such a diverting confrontation. He centered his poem on the relics, while probably, in addition to the *Descriptio*, using an existing epic tradition of a military expedition led by Charlemagne against Constantinople (see J. Horrent, 1960; P. Aebischer, 1956, p. 161). The fact that the poet did not mention the fragment of the Cross among the relics owned by Saint-Denis seems to be a clear indication that he did not want to take sides in the conflict. However, as we have seen, his poem is not a satire of the relics; it is a tongue-in-cheek comment on the continuing rivalry. As noted by Horrent (1961, p. 116), the poet "does not believe in what he is telling and does not really want his public to believe in it."

The Bishop's participation in the *Lendit* of the Plaine-Saint-Denis did not stop in 1124, and the rivalry continued for a long time afterward. As noted by Levillain (p. 272), it seems to have flared up again at the beginning of the thirteenth century. At that time, Baudouin, the Latin Emperor of Constantinople, presented King Philip Augustus with relics from the Imperial Chapel of Bucoleon. The King in turn gave these relics—among them was a fragment of the True Cross—to the Royal Abbey of Saint-Denis on June 7, 1205. Though the monks of Saint-Denis already owned a fragment of the Cross, the King's gift is likely to have rekindled the competition. "There is no doubt that this fragment of the Cross of Golgotha, extraordinary by its dimensions, was capable of creating a disastrous competition against the fragment from the same cross in the Paris cathedral" (Levillain, p. 272).

Dating

The *Voyage* was written at some point during this long period of rivalry, which lasted from about 1109 until shortly after 1205. Linguistic studies of the poem have not resulted in a more accurate dating of this work. They have produced datings varying from the second half of the eleventh century (Koschwitz) to the second half of the thirteenth century (Favati, 1965).

Unity of the "Voyage"

In the nineteenth century, critics thought that the *Voyage* was based on a number of different stories. They felt that the tone of the Jerusalem episode clashed with that taking place in Constantinople. This opinion has been largely superseded by the view that the *Voyage* shows much cohesion (one conspicuous exception: J. Rychner, 1955). The *Voyage* may not have a plot that is as tightly-knit as the *Roland*, but that work is unique. As we have seen, Latin works suggested its two major themes: Charlemagne's journey to Jerusalem, and his journey to Constantinople. In the *Voyage*, the reason for his visit to these two cities has been harmonized. For example, in the second scene (58-75), Charlemagne is goaded by the Queen to go to Constantinople to confront the Emperor of the East, but he also mentions Jerusalem as the main goal of his journey (67-71). Later, in Jerusalem, Charlemagne tells the Patriarch that he will journey to Constantinople to look for a thirteenth king whom he must defeat (153). He also remembers the Queen's words (234). When he is in Constantinople, he tells Hugo that he comes from Jerusalem and is returning to France (308). At the end of the poem, these elements are alluded to and skillfully meshed when Charlemagne forgives the Queen in honor of the Holy Sepulchre where he has worshipped (869-870). But the most single important link between both themes is provided by the relics. They are given to Charlemagne by the Patriarch in Jerusalem, where they perform great miracles (192-195). In Constantinople, when the Emperor and his men are forced to perform their boasts, the relics are brought to them (667) and help, indirectly, the beleaguered Frenchmen. Finally, when the French are back home, the relics are divided and distributed throughout France, except for the Nail and the Crown of Thorns which are given to Saint-Denis (866-867).

It should be emphasized that the serious and pious atmosphere in the episodes taking place in Jerusalem, does not clash with the light and humorous ambiance prevailing in Constantinople. In the former city, the pious behavior of the French and the serenity of their presence in the church of Jerusalem are offset by the appearance of the Jew (129-140), while in the latter city, the comical climate also includes the sincere repentance of the French, followed by the intervention of an angel sent by God (668-677). As Horrent (1959, p. 417) pointed out: "He (the poet) has had a constant concern to blend the various parts in a coherent whole, and to establish visible links between them." Such care suggests careful planning.

Composition of the Poem

As pointed out by J. Rychner (1955, pp. 114-115) and developed by J. Horrent (1959, pp. 419-427), the narrative units of the *Voyage* do not correspond, generally, with the *laisses*; they overlap. For example, the opening scene involving Charlemagne and the Queen extends from the first *laisse* through the fourth. This characteristic does not mean that the poet lacks skill; quite the contrary. He uses this technique throughout his poem to give it more fluidity. When he decides to slow down the narrative, he changes to the true epic *laisse*. In the comic episode of the boasts (453-617), the poet has recourse to this technique with great success. The *laisses* of that passage are narratively independent and set off better the comic elements of each boast.

This brief analysis of the composition of the *Voyage* shows that the poet was a skilled artist conscious of the techniques that he used to enhance his entertaining story.

Text and Translation

About half a dozen different titles have been used for the *Voyage*, among them, *Le Pèlerinage de Charlemagne à Jérusalem et à Constantinople* (*The Pilgrimage of Charlemagne to Jerusalem and Constantinople*), first employed by G. Paris; and *Le Voyage de Charlemagne à Jérusalem et à Constantinople* (*The Journey of Charlemagne to Jerusalem and Constantinople*), first given by P. Paris in 1859. Each title implies a certain interpretation of the poem. It seems logical to have a title which respects the French incipit: *Ci comence le livre cumment Charles de Fraunce voiet in Jerusalem et, pur paroles sa feme, a Constantinnoble, pur ver roy Hugon.* As P. Aebischer (1965, p. 15) has pointed out, one of the key words of the original title is the verbal form *voiet*, from the infinitive *voier*, "to travel." The term for pilgrimage does not appear here.

The poem was preserved in a single manuscript, in the British Museum until 1879 or 1880, when it disappeared. This version of the *Voyage* had probably been copied in the fourteenth century by an Anglo-Norman scribe who did not seem to be too familiar with the French used by the original author—who probably lived on the Continent—especially with the rules of versification. The manuscript was first edited and published in 1836 by Francisque Michel under the title *Charlemagne, an Anglo-Norman Poem of the Twelfth Century*. In 1879, E. Koschwitz published the poem as *Karls des Grossen Reise nach Jerusalem und Constantinopel*. It was corrected and printed seven times, until 1923. The German medievalist's work was based on Michel's edition, which had been collated on the original by R. P. Wülcker, and on a "fascimile" prepared by J. Koch. In a review of Koschwitz' first edition, H. Nicol stated that he had collated the text with the original manuscript and that he had noted only a few minor errors. Koschwitz provided a diplomatic transcript of the *Voyage*, which is today the only text available for a critical edition of the poem.

Given this situation, it is no surprise that the various editions of the poem, including the more recent ones by P. Aebischer (1965) and G. Favati (1965), offer corrections and emendations that are sometimes at considerable variance. For this reason, we have selected readings from all existing editions in order to produce the new text. Also of great use were M. Tyssens' comments (1978), and J. Horrent's textual notes (1961). Our own readings and emendations are few (193, 273, 288, 314, 315, 466, 479, 676, 820, 822, 852). Because of the nature of the present work, we have not attempted to give the variant readings found in all existing editions. Only the most problematic cases have been indicated in the text with an asterisk and discussed in the *Notes*. We have given, in footnotes, the rejected readings, and solved the abbreviations according to the usual editorial rules: *i* has been distinguished from *j*, *u* from *v*; the acute accent has been used on stressed final *e*; also the cedilla under *c* indicates the *s* sound. We have used the diaeresis sparingly. We have not interfered with the scribe's orthography, for example the final *z* often used for *t*. We have maintained his confusion of the subject and the oblique cases. Emendations of the text have been kept to a minimum. Only syntactically and metrically incorrect verses have been corrected.

The *Voyage* was translated, or rather adapted, into English by M. Sherwood and published in 1927 under the title of *The Merry Pilgrimage*. The translation itself is written in a style typical of the translations of medieval literature done at the beginning of this century. Short passages were occasionally left out and there are a number of inaccuracies. The whole episode relating to Oliver's relationship with Hugo's daughter was omitted. Explanatory passages were added, most notably a short conclusion to the poem.

In this prose translation, we have endeavored to remain as close as possible to the original, while using contemporary English. Archaic or uncommon terms are defined in the *Notes*. Old French authors often changed tenses, switching especially from present to past, and vice versa. We have maintained the original tenses in most cases. At times, due to the nature of Old French syntax, the sentence pattern and the punctuation of the translation depart from the original French text.

I wish to express my thanks to Walter Langlois of the University of Wyoming, to John L. Grigsby of Washington University, and to Gerard J. Brault of Pennsylvania State University for reading my manuscript and offering numerous valuable suggestions. I also wish to thank the editor of Summa Publications, N. J. Lacy, for his assistance. I gratefully acknowledge the substantial grant from the College of Arts and Sciences of the University of Wyoming which made the publication of this work possible. A special word of thanks goes to my wife, Rita, who prepared the manuscript with the help of the computer.

THE JOURNEY OF CHARLEMAGNE

Ci comence le livere cumment Charles de Fraunce voiet in Jerusalem et, pur paroles sa feme, a Constantinnoble, pur ver roy Hugon.

I

    Un jur fu li reis Karles* al Seint Denis muster; (1)
Reout prise sa corune, en croiz seignat sun chef,
E ad ceinte s'espee dunt li ponz fud d'or mer. (3)
Dux i out et demeines, baruns e chevalers. (4)
5   Charles li empereres reguardet sa muiller: (5)
Ele fut corunee al plus bel e al meuz. (6)
Il la prist par le poin desuz un oliver,
De sa pleine parole la prist a reisuner*:
"Dame veïstes unkes hume nul desuz ceil (9)
10   Tant ben seïst espee ne la corone el chef?
Uncor cunquerrei jo citez ot mun espez*!" (11)
Cele ne fud pas sage, folement respondeit:
"Emperere," dist ele, "trop vus pöez preiser;
Uncore en sai jo un ki plus se fait leger (14)
15   Quant il porte corune entre ses chevalers:
Kaunt la met sur sa teste, plus belement lui set!" (16)
Quant l'entend li reis* Charles, mult en est curecez; (17)
Pur Franceis ki l'oïrent, mult en est enbrunchez. (18)
"E, dame, u est cil reis? Kar vus le m'enseinez! (19)
20   Si porterum ensemble les corunes as cheis;

Rejected Readings

Incipit: c. charels de; pur perols; pur verer roy
        (1) fu karleun al s. d.
        (3) sa espee li ponz
        (4) demeines e baruns
        (5) Li empereres r. la reine sa muillers
        (6) fut ben corunee; e as meuz
        (9) nul dedesuz ceil
        (11) Uncore cunquerrei; espeez
        (14) en sa jo
        (16) Kaunt il la met
        (17) lentend charle mult est c.
        (18) mult est e.
        (19) Kar le menseinez

Here Begins the Book on how Charles of France Journeys to Jerusalem and, because of his Spouse's Words, to Constantinople, to Meet with King Hugo.

I

    One day King Charles was at the church of Saint-Denis.
He had put his crown back on his head; he made the sign of the cross
And he girded on his sword whose pommel was of pure gold. (3)
Dukes, lords, barons and knights were all there.
5   Emperor Charles looked at his spouse:
No one bore a crown better than she.
He took her by the hand beneath an olive tree
And, with a firm voice, he began to speak to her:
"Lady, have you ever seen a man on earth
10   Wearing such a fitting sword and crown?
With my spear I shall still conquer many cities!"
She was not very wise and, without thinking, answered:
"Emperor," said she, "you hold yourself in too high esteem;
I know of one who has more presence than you
15   When wearing his crown amidst his knights:
It befits him better when he places it on his head!"
When King Charles hears her, he becomes filled with wrath;
He keeps his head bowed because the Frenchmen have heard her.
"Tell me, lady, where is that king? I want you to tell me!
20   Side by side will he and I wear our crowns;

Si i serrunt vos druz e tuz vos cunsilers;
Jo maunderai ma court de mes bons chevalers.
Si Franceis le me dïent, dunc lur otri jo ben; (23)
Se vus m'avez mentid, vus le cumperez cher: (24)
25 Trencherai vus la teste od m'espee d'acer." (25)
"Emperere," dist ele, "ne vus en curucez!
Plus est riche d'aver e d'or e de deners, (27)
Mais n'est mie si pruz ne si bon chevalers
Pur ferir en bataile ne pur i encaucer." (29)
30 Quant ce out la reïne ke Charle est si irrez, (30)
Forment s'en repent ele, vuelt li chaïr as pez. (31)

II

"Emperere," dist ele, "mercid pur amur Deu! (32)
Ja sui ge vostre femme, si me quidai jüer; (33)
Jo m'escundirai ja, se vus le cumandez, (34)
35 A jurer serement u juïse a porter:
De la plus haulte tur de Paris la citez
Me larrai cuntreval par creant devaler, (37)
Que pur la vostre hunte ne fud dit ne pensed."
"Nu ferez," ço dist Charle, "mais le rei me numez!" (39)
40 "Emperere," dist ele, "ja nel puis jo truver."
"Par mun chef," ço dist Carle, "orendreit lem dirrez, (41)
U jo vus ferai ja cele teste couper!" (42)

---

(23) dunc le otri
(24) me avez m.
(25) me espee
(27) de aver dor
(29) pur encaucer
(30) ke charle est
(31) sen repent vuelt
(32) Empere
(33) Ja su ge
(34) mescundirari
(37) par creance d.
(39) Nu frez dist ch.
(41) chef dist c.; le me dirrez
(42) vus frai ja

Your trusted friends and all your advisers will be there;
As for me, I shall summon the good knights of my court;
If the Frenchmen agree with you, then I shall accept their opinion;
But if you have lied to me, then you will pay dearly for it:
25 I shall behead you with my steel blade."
"Emperor," said she, "do not be angry with me because of this!
Though he has more riches, gold and pieces of silver than you,
He is not as valiant as you, nor is he as good a knight
For smiting in battle and for pressing hard the enemy."
30 When the Queen hears that Charles is so vexed,
She is very sorry for it, and she would throw herself at his feet.

II

"Emperor," said she, "I beg your mercy for God's love!
In spite of all that I have said, I am still your wife; I thought
    I was merely jesting;
If you order it, I shall exonerate myself now,
35 Either by swearing an oath or by undergoing an ordeal.
To bear testimony that I did not say it nor think it to disgrace you,
I shall throw myself down
From the highest tower in the city of Paris."
"No, you will not," said Charles; "give me instead the name of
    that king!"
40 "Emperor," said she, "in truth I cannot think of it."
"I swear by this head of mine," said Charles, "either you tell
    me at once,
Or I shall have you immediately beheaded!"

III

Ore entend la reïne que ne se puet estordre*; (43)
Volenters la leisast, mais que müer nen osed. (44)
45 "Emperere," dist ele, "ne me tenez a fole;
Del rei Hugun le Fort ai mult oï parole:
Emperere est de Grece e de Costuntinoble;
Il tent trestute Perse tresque en Capadoce. (48)
N'at tant bel chevaler de ci en Antioche;
50 Onc ne fut tel barnez cum le sun, senz le vostre." (50)
"Par mun chef," ço dist Carle, "ço savrai jo uncore! (51)
Se mençunge avez dite, a fiance estes morte!"

IV

"Par ma fei," dist li reis, "mult m'aveiz irascud;
M'amisted e mun gred en avez tut perduz.
55 Uncor quid qu'en perdrez la teste sur le buc. (55)
Nel dusés ja penser, dame, de ma vertuz! (56)
Ja n'en prendrai mais fin tresque l'avrei veüz!" (57)

V

L'emperere de France, cum il fud curunez (58)
E out faite s'offrende a l'auter principel, (59)
60 A la sale a Parys si s'en est retornez. (60)
Rolland et Oliver en ad ot sei menez, (61)
E Willeme d'Orenge et Naimon l'adurez, (62)
Oger de Denemarche, Gerin et Berenger*, (63)

---

(43) puet estorcer
(44) Volenteres
(48) tent tute perse
(50) Ne fut
(51) chef dist carle ço saverai
(55) Uncore; perderez
(56) Ne duses; dame du ma v.
(57) prenderari; laverei veuz
(58) Li emperere
(59) sa offrende
(60) sale de parys
(61) sei amenez
(62) de orenge
(63) denemarche Berin

III

    The Queen understands now that she cannot evade.
    She would have gladly dropped the matter, except that she did not
        dare change what she had said.
45 "Emperor," said she, "do not think that I have lost my mind;
    I have heard much about King Hugo the Strong:
    He is Emperor of Greece and Constantinople,
    And he rules all of Persia as far as Cappadocia;
    There is not as handsome a knight from here to Antioch;
50 Except for yours, never has there been nobility like his." (50)
    "By this head of mine," said Charles, "I shall certainly find out!
    If you have told me a lie, you can be sure to die!"

IV

    "By my faith," said the King, "you have filled me with wrath;
    Because of this, you have lost my friendship and favor;
55 I doubt that your head shall long remain on your shoulders.
    Lady, you should not have thought so poorly of my power!
    I shall have no rest until I have seen this king!"

V

    The Emperor of France—after he had put his crown on his head
    And made his offering at the main altar—
60 Returned to his palace in Paris.
    With him he has taken Roland and Oliver,
    William of Orange and Naimes the Valiant,
    Ogier of Denmark, Gerin and Berengier,

L'arceveske Turpin, Ernalz et Haïmer, (64)
65   E Bernard de Brusban, et Bertram l'adurez, (65)
     E tel .M. chevaler ki sunt de France nez.
     "Seignors," dist l'emperere, "un petit m'entendez:
     En un lointain rëaume, si Deu pleist, en irrez
     Jerusalem requere, la terre Damnedeu. (69)
70   La Croiz et le Sepulcre voil aler aürer: (70)
     Jo l'ai trei feiz sunged, moi i covent aler;
     Irrai un rei requerre, dount ai oï parler. (72)
     Set .C. cameilz merrez, d'or et d'argent trussed, (73)
     Pur set aunz en la tere ester e demurer; (74)
75   Ja ne m'en turnerai trescque l'avrai trovez." (75)

VI

     L'emperere de France feit cunreer sa gent: (76)
     Ceols qui od lui alerent cunreat gentement; (77)
     Asez lur ad donez entre or fin et argent. (78)
     N'i unt escuz ne lances ne espees trenchaunz,
80   Meis fustz feret de fraine et escrepes pendanz;
     N'i funt ferrer destrés ne detrés ne deuvant*: (81)
     Les mulz e les sumers afeutrent li servant,
     E funt pleines les males entre or fin et argent,
     De veisaus, de deners et d'autre garnement; (84)
85   Faudestoulz d'or i portent et treis de seie blanc.
     A Seint Denis de France li reis s'escrepe prent;
     L'arcevesche Turpin li seignat gentement, (87)
     E si prist il la sue, e Franceis ensement,

---

(64) Le arceveske t. et ernalz
(65) bernand; Berteram
(69) requere et la mere d.
(70) et la sepulcre
(72) E irrai
(73) de argent
(74) ester u demurer
(75) laverari trovez
(76) Li emperere
(77) E ceols qui alerent od lui
(78) entrere or
(81) E funt f. les d. de tres et de uvant
(84) veisaus et de d. et de autre
(87) Li arcevesche

       The Archbishop Turpin, Ernaut and Aïmer,
65   And Bernard of Brusban, and Bertrand the Valiant,
       And a thousand such knights who were born in France.
       "My lords," said the Emperor, "listen to me for a moment:
       God willing, you will go to a distant kingdom
       To seek Jerusalem, the land of our Lord God;
70   I want to go there to worship the Cross and the Sepulchre:
       I dreamed of it three times, thus I am bound to go there; (71)
       I shall look for a king about whom I have heard.
       In order to stay and live for seven years in that land,
       You will take along seven hundred camels laden with gold and
             silver; (74)
75   I shall never return until I have found him."

VI

       The Emperor of France has his men arrayed;
       He provided generously for those who were to go with him;
       He bestowed large gifts on them, both of fine gold and silver.
       They carry no shields, or lances or sharp swords,
80   But iron-shod staffs of ashwood, and dangling scrips; (80)
       They do not have war-horses shod in front and behind;
       The servants are harnessing the mules and the sumpters, (82)
       And they are filling the chests with both fine gold and silver,
       With vessels, pieces of silver, and other equipment;
85   They are taking along folding seats of gold and tents of white silk.
       At Saint-Denis of France the King gets his scrip;
       Archbishop Turpin blessed it solemnly,
       And then he took his own, and so did all the Frenchmen;

E munterent as mulz qu'orent forz et amblanz. (89)
90 De la citez isirent, si s'en turnent brochaunt. (90)
Des or s'en irrat Carles al Damnedeu cummant. (91)
La reïne remeint, doloruse et pluraunt.
Tant chevauchet li reis qu'il en vint en un plain; (93)
A une part s'en turnet, si apelet Bertram: (94)
95 "Veez gentes cumpaines de pelerins erraund! (95)
Hitantes milies sunt el premer chef devant: (96)
Ki ço duit e governet ben deit estre poant!"

VII

Or vait li emperere od ses granz cumpainies. (98)
Devant el premer chef furent oitante milie. (99)
100 Il issirent de France et Burgoine guerpirent*,
Loheregne traversent, Baivere et Hungerie,
Les Turcs et les Persaunz, et cele gent haïe;
La grant ewe del flum passerent a Lalice. (103)
Chevauchet li emperere tres par mi Croiz partie,
105 Les bois et les forez, et sunt entrez en Grice; (105)
Les puis et les muntaines virent en Romanie,
E brochent a la terre u Deus receut martirie.
Veient Jerusalem, une citez antive:
Li jours fu beaus et clers; herberges unt purprises,
110 E venent al muster, offrendes i unt mises; (110)
As herberges repairent les feres cumpainies.

---

(89) E muntent; quil orent
(90) citez en isirent
(91) Des ore; cales a damne Deu le c.
(93) quil vint
(94) berteraram
(95) Veez cum gentes
(96) E hitantes
(98) Ore
(99) oitante milz
(103) passerent a la liee
(105) en grece
(110) lur offerendes

　　　　Then they mounted their mules which were strong and ambling;
 90　They rode out of the city and spurred on their way.
　　　　From then Charles will go onward, with God's help;
　　　　The Queen remains behind, afflicted and weeping.
　　　　The King rides so long that he comes to a plain;
　　　　There he turns away and calls Bertrand:
 95　"Behold these noble companies of journeying pilgrims!
　　　　In the vanguard alone there are eighty thousand of them:
　　　　How mighty must be the one who is leading and governing them!"

VII

　　　　Now the Emperor is riding on with his large companies;
　　　　In the vanguard alone there were eighty thousand men;
100　They rode out of France and left Burgundy behind, (100)
　　　　They are riding through Lorraine, Bavaria, and Hungary;
　　　　They find their way through the Turks and the Persians,
　　　　　　and through the hated race;
　　　　At Laodicea they crossed over the great water of the river;
　　　　The Emperor is riding onward deep into the region of the Cross,
105　Into the woods and the forests, and then they came to Greece;
　　　　In Romany they saw the hilltops and the mountains,
　　　　And now they are spurring forward to the land where Christ
　　　　　　was martyred.
　　　　At last they discern Jerusalem, an ancient city:
　　　　That day was fine and bright; they set up their quarters,
110　And next they go to church to make their offerings;
　　　　Afterwards these valiant companies go back to their camp.

VIII

Mult est genz li presenz que reis Carles i offret. (112)
Entrat en un muster de marbre peint a volte:
Laens ad un alter de Saincte Paternostre:
115 Deus i chantat la messe, si firent li apostle; (115)
E les .XII. chaeres i sunt tutes uncore:
La trezime est en mi, ben seelee et close. (117)
Cum Karle i entrat, ben out al queor grant joie: (118)
Cum il vit la chaere, icele part s'aprocet: (119)
120 L'emperere s'asist, un petit se reposet, (120)
Li .XII. pers as altres, envirunt e en coste; (121)
Ainz nen i sist nuls hume, ne unkes pus uncore. (122)

IX

Mult fu let li reis Karles de cele grant bealté. (123)
Vit de cleres colurs li muster peinturez, (124)
125 De martirs et de virgines et de grant majestez,
E les curs de la lune et les festes anuels,
E les lavacres curre et les peisons par mer.
Karles out fer le vis, si out le chef levez.
Uns Judeus i entrat, ki ben l'out esgardet:
130 Cum il vit le rei Karle, cumençat a trembler: (130)
Tant out fer le visage, ne l'osat esgarder:
A poi que il ne chet, fuant s'en est turnet,
E si muntet d'elais tuz les marbrins degrez,
Si vint al patriarche, prist l'en a a parler: (134)

---

(112) qui carles
(115) chantat messe
(117) La treezime
(118) Karle i.e. Cum *is missing.*
(119) si aprocet
(120) Li emperere
(121) peers
(122) Ainz ni sist hume
(123) let karles
(124) depeinturez
(130) vit karle
(134) Vint al p.; len a parler

VIII

The present that King Charles gives there is very valuable.
He entered a marble church with painted vaults:
Inside there is an altar dedicated to Holy Paternoster:
115 God celebrated mass there, and so did the Apostles;
And all twelve seats are still there:
The thirteenth stands in the center, well sealed and closed off. (117)
When Charlemagne walked in, his heart was filled with joy:
When he saw the seat, he went up to it:
120 The Emperor sat down in it and rested a little,
And so did the Twelve Peers on the other seats, all around him; (121)
No man had ever sat there before, and no one since.

IX

King Charles was very pleased with the great beauty of the church.
He saw that it was painted with bright colors,
125 With martyrs, virgins, and great Majesties, (125)
With the phases of the moon and the solemn feasts,
With the baptismal water running, and with the fishes in the sea;
Charles' face was proud and he was holding his head high.
A Jew who had watched attentively walked in;
130 Upon seeing King Charles, he began to tremble:
Charles' face was so proud that he did not dare look at him:
He almost fell down; then he turned and took to flight;
He climbed up the marble steps all at once,
And hurried to the Patriarch; he then began to speak to him:

The Journey of Charlemagne

135 "Alez, sire, al muster pur les funz aprester; (135)
Orendreit me ferai baptizer et lever! (136)
Duze cuntes vi ore en cel muster entrer, (137)
Oveoc euls le trezime, unc ne vi si formet.
Par le men escïentre, ço est meïmes Deus!
140 Il et li duze apostle vus venent visiter!"
Quant l'ot li patriarche, si s'en vait cunreer,
E out mandet ses clers en albe en la citet*; (142)
Il les feit revestir et capes afubler.
A grant procession en est al rei alet.
145 L'emperere le vit, s'est cuntre lui levet; (145)
E out trait sun capel, parfunt lui a clinet. (146)
Vunt sei entrebaiser, nuveles demander, (147)
E dist li patriarche: "Dunt estes, sire, nez? (148)
Unkes mais n'osat hoem en cest muster entrer, (149)
150 Si ne li comandai u ne li oi ruvet."
"Sire, jo ai nun Karle, si sui de France nez. (151)
Duze reis ai cunquis par force et par barnez;
Li trezime vois querre, dunt ai oï parler;
Vinc en Jerusalem pur l'amistet de Deu;
155 La Croiz e le Sepulcre sui venuz aürer."
E dist li patriarches: "Sire, mult estes ber: (156)
Sis as en la chaere u sist meïmes Deus: (157)
Aies nun Charles Maines* sur tuz reis curunez!" (158)
E dist li emperere: "Cin cenz merciz de Deu!
160 De voz saintes reliques, si vus plaist, me donez,
Que porterai en France, qu'en voil enluminer."
Respont li patriarches: "A plentet en avrez: (162)

---

(135) musterer
(136) me frai b.
(137) musterer
(142) albe la citet
(145) Li emperere; si est encuntre lui
(146) out taat sun c.
(147) Vunt entrebaiser
(148) neez
(149) mais ne nosat
(151) neez
(156) beer
(157) sist mames d.
(158) charles sur tuz
(162) averez

135 "Sire, hasten to the church to prepare the fonts:
    I now want to be baptized and cleansed!
    I just saw there twelve counts walk in this church,
    And with them was a thirteenth: never did I see such a handsome man;
    By my faith, it is God himself!
140 He and the Twelve Apostles are coming to pay you a visit!"
    Upon hearing him, the Patriarch goes to put on his vestment,
    And sends, throughout the city, for his clerks with their albs; (142)
    He bids them to don their vestments and their copes. (143)
    The Patriarch then went to the King in a long procession;
145 The Emperor saw him and rose to meet him;
    He took off his headgear and bowed deeply to him;
    They embrace each other and ask about the state of affairs,
    And the Patriarch said: "Where were you born, Sire?
    No one before ever dared enter this church,
150 Unless I had ordered it or asked."
    "Sire, my name is Charles, and I was born in France;
    I conquered twelve kings by my might and prowess,
    And I am on my way to seek the thirteenth, of whom I have heard;
    I have come to Jerusalem for the love of God;
155 I have come here to worship the Cross and the Sepulchre."
    And the Patriarch said: "Sire, you are very valiant indeed:
    You have sat in the very seat where God himself sat:
    Therefore call yourself Charlemagne, great above all crowned kings!"
    And the Emperor said: "In God's name, I thank you five hundred times!
160 If it pleases you, give me some of your holy relics: (160)
    I shall bring them back to France, which I wish to enlighten."
    The Patriarch answers: "You will have plenty:

Le braz saint Simeon aparmaines avrez, (163)
E le chef saint Lazare vus ferai aporter, (164)
165 E del sanc saint Estefne, ki martir fu pur Deu." (165)
Karlemaines l'en rent saluz et amistez.

X

E dist li patriarches: "Ben avez espleitez
Quan Deus venistes querre: estre vus dait le melz.
Durrai vus tels reliques, meilurs nen ad suz cel:
170 Del sudarie Jhesu que il out en sun chef (170)
Cum il fu al sepulcre et poset et colchet—
Quant Judeus le garderent as espees d'ascer, (172)
Al terz jur relevat, cum il out predicet, (173)
E il vint as apostles pur euls esleecer—; (174)
175 E un des clous avrez que il out en sun ped, (175)
E la sainte corone que Deus out en sun chef,
E avrez le calice que il beneïsquied; (177)
L'esqüele d'argent vus durrai volenters: (178)
Entailee est a or et a peres preciels; (179)
180 E avrez le cultel que Deus tint al manger, (180)
De la barbe saint Pere, des chevols de sun chef." (181)
Karlemaines l'en rent saluz et amistez:
Tut li cors li tressalt de joie et de pitez.

XI

Ço dist li patriarche: "Ben vus est avenuz;
185 Par le men escïentre, Deus vus i a cundust! (185)

---

(163) a par mames en averez
(164) vus frai a.
(165) Del sanc
(170) Dul sudarie
(172) de ascer
(173) relevat si cum
(174) eslecer
(175) Un des clous averez
(177) E averez; benesquid
(178) La esquele de argent
(179) peres precioses
(180) E averez
(181) pere et des chevols
(185) acundustid. *The last two letters are expunged.*

    For the time being you will have Saint Simon's arm,
    And I shall send for Saint Lazarus' head
165 And for some of Saint Stephen's blood, who was martyred for God."
    In return Charlemagne extends to him his greetings and his friendship.

X

    Then the Patriarch said: "You acted wisely
    When you came to pay a visit to God: it should bring you good fortune;
    I shall give you relics such that there are none better on earth:
170 A piece of Jesus' shroud that was on His head
    When He was laid down in the sepulchre—
    While the Jews were keeping watch with their swords of steel,
    On the third day He rose from the dead, as He had predicted,
    And went to the Apostles to make them rejoice—
175 Also you will have one of the nails which went through His foot,
    And the Holy Crown that God wore on His head,
    And you will have the chalice that He blessed;
    I shall gladly give you the silver bowl:
    It is inlaid with gold and precious stones;
180 You will have the knife that God used for His meal,
    And also something of Saint Peter's beard, with some of his hair."
    In return Charlemagne extends to him his greetings and his friendship:
    He is thrilled with joy and sympathy.

XI

    The Patriarch said: "You have good fortune;
185 By my faith, it is God who has led you here!

Durrai vus tels reliques ke ferunt grant vertuz: (186)
Del leyt sainte Marie dunt aleytat Jhesus, (187)
Cum fud primes en terre entre nus decendut;
De la sainte chemise que ele out revestut."
190 Karlemaines l'en rent amistet et saluz.
Cil li fist aporter, et li reis les reçut.
Les reliques sunt forz, Deus i fait grant vertuz:
Iloc juit un contrait, set anz out ke ne mut; (193)
Tut li os li crussirent, li ners li sunt tendut: (194)
195 Ore sailt sus en pez, unkes plus sain ne fud. (195)
Or veit li patriarches Deus i fait grant vertut: (196)
Tost fait le glas suner par la citet menut.
Li reis fait faire un fertre, unkes meldre ne fud; (198)
Del plus fin or d'Arabie i out mil mars fundud.
200 Il l'a fait seieler a force et a vertuz, (200)
A grant bendes d'argent l'a fait lïer menuz; (201)
L'erceveske Turpin comandet seit cundut. (202)
Karlemaines fud lez et tuz qui sunt od lui. (203)

XII

Quatre mais fud li reis en Jersalem la vile;
205 Il et li duze per, la chere cumpanie, (205)
Demeinent grant barnage, car l'emperere est riche. (206)
Comencent un muster k'est de sainte Marie: (207)
Li hume de la terre la claiment la Latine, (208)
Car li language i venet de trestute la vile;

---

(186) ke teles r. ke frunt grant
(187) dunt ele aleytat
(193) ne se mut
(194) sunt estendut
(195) en peez
(196) Ore; fait vertut
(198) faire une fertere
(200) seiler
(201) de argent; fait il lier
(202) A lerceveske; comandet que seit
(203) tuz icil que sunt
(205) Il et duze par
(206) car li emperere
(207) ke est
(208) la latanie

I shall give you relics that will perform great miracles:
Some milk from Saint Mary, with which she nursed Jesus
When He first came down on earth amidst us;
Also a piece of the holy shift that she wore." (189)
190 In return Charlemagne extends to him his greetings and his friendship.
The Patriarch had the relics brought, and the King accepted them;
They are powerful; through them God performs great miracles:
A lame man was lying there; he had not moved in seven years;
All his joints cracked, his muscles contracted:
195 He then leapt back on his feet; never had he been more healthy.
Now the Patriarch sees that God has performed a great miracle:
Immediately he calls for the church bells to chime, throughout the city.
The King has a reliquary made, never was there a better one;
A thousand marks of the finest gold from Arabia were melted down for it; (199)
200 He then had it sealed securely
And bound closely with large silver bands;
He calls for it to be brought to Archbishop Turpin.
Charlemagne was joyful, and all those who were with him.

XII

The King remained in the city of Jerusalem four months;
205 He and the Twelve Peers, his beloved company, (205)
Live in true magnificence, for the Emperor is wealthy;
They found a church dedicated to Saint Mary:
The men of this land call it the "Latin,"
Because, throughout the city, people of many nationalities go there (209)

210 Il i vendent lur pailes, lur teiles et lur siries, (210)
    Coste, canele, peivre, altres bones espices (211)
    E maintes bones herbes que jo ne vus sai dire.
    Deus est uncore el cel quin volt faire justise! (213)

XIII

    L'emperere de France i out tant demuret, (214)
215 Li patriarche prist, si l'en ad apelet:
    "Vostre cunget, bael sire, si vus plaist me donet:
    En France, a mun rëalme, m'en estut returner;
    Pose at que jo n'i fui, si ai mult demurret, (218)
    E ne set mis barnages quel part jo sui turnet.
220 Faites .C. mulz receivre d'or et d'argent trusset." (220)
    E dist li patriarches: "Ja mar en parlerez! (221)
    Tuz li mens granz tresors vus seit abandunez: (222)
    Tant en prengent Franceis cum en vuldrent porter,
    Mais que de Sarazins, de paiens vus gardet, (224)
225 Qui nus volent destrure sainte Cristïentez!" (225)

XIV

    E dist li patriarches: "Savez dunt jo vus priz*?
    De Sarazins destrure, ki nus ount en despit."
    "Volenters," ço dist Karles. Sa fei si l'en plevit. (228)

XV

    "Jo manderrai mes humes, quant qu'en purrai aver,
230 E irrai en Espaine, ne purat remaner."

---

(210) lur series
(211) Coste et c. peivere et a.
(213) cel que en volt
(214) Li emperere
(218) Posat
(220) receivere
(221) ja ma en
(222) vus seint a.
(224) sarazins et de p.
(225) destrure et sainte c.
(228) Volenteres

210 To sell their silk cloth, their linen cloth, and their damasks, (210)
Also costmary, cinnamon, pepper, other fine spices, (211)
And many a good herb, the names of which I do not know;
But there is still a God in heaven who will attend to all this! (213)

XIII

The Emperor of France remained there so long
215 That he took the Patriarch aside and addressed him thus:
"Fair Sire, pray give me your leave:
To my kingdom, to France, must I return;
I have now been away for some time; I have tarried here too long,
And my barons do not know where I am.
220 Order that one hundred of my mules, packed with gold and silver, be given to you."
But the Patriarch said: "I could not think of it!
Rather I leave all my vast treasure to you:
Let the Frenchmen take as much of it as they wish to carry,
Provided that you guard yourself against the Saracens and the Pagans
225 Who want to destroy our Holy Christendom."

XIV

And the Patriarch said: "Do you understand what I am asking you to do?
To crush the Saracens who profess hatred against us."
"I shall gladly," said Charles; and he pledged his faith.

XV

"I shall summon my liegemen, all those whom I shall be able to gather,
230 And I shall go into Spain, without hesitation." (230)

Si fist il pus encore, ben en gardat sa fei, (231)
Quant la fud mort Rollant, li .XII. per od sei. (232)

XVI

L'emperere de France i out tant demured, (233)
De sa muller li membret, ke il oït parler: (234)
235 Ore irrat lu rei querre, qu'ele li out löet: (235)
Ja n'en prendrat mais fin tresqu'il l'avrat trovet. (236)
La nuit le fait nuncier as Franceis as ostels:
Cum il l'unt entendut, orent le quer mult lez. (238)
Al matin par sum l'albe, quant li jurz lur apert, (239)
240 Li mul et li sumer sunt garniz et trusset;
E muntent li barun, el chimin sunt entret;
Venent en Jerico, palmes prenent aset. (242)
"Utree, Deus aïe!" crient et halt et cler. (243)
Li patriarches muntet sur un mulz sujurnez;
245 Tant cum li jurz li duret l'at cunduz e guïez.
La nuit furent ensenble li baruns as ostels:
Nule ren qu'il demandent ne lur est demuret. (247)
Al matin par sum l'albe, quant li jurs lur apert,
Remuntent li barun, al chemin sunt entret.
250 Li patriarches ad Karlemaine apelet:
"Vostre cungé, bels sire, si vus plaist me donez." (251)
E dist li emperere: "Al cumant Damnedeu!" (252)
Vunt saei entrebaiser, atant sunt desevret. (253)
Chevauchet l'emperere od sun ruiste barnet. (254)

---

(231) pus car ben
(232) rollant et li .XII. per
(233) Li emperere
(234) li mendret ke il out p.
(235) que ele
(236) prenderat; laverat
(238) e. si orent le queres m. leez
(239) matin sum la lalbe
(242) palmes i p.
(243) Utre
(247) ren que il
(251) cunge si vus p.
(252) lemperere
(253) deseveret
(254) li emperere

So did he afterwards, indeed keeping his pledge,
Considering that Roland was slain there, together with the Twelve Peers.

XVI

The Emperor of France remained there so long
That he eventually remembered the words spoken by his wife.
235 So now he will go and look for the king she had praised:
He will not rest till he has found him.
That night he has the news announced to his Frenchmen in their lodgings:
When they heard him, their hearts rejoiced.
In the morning, at dawn, when they perceive daylight,
240 The mules and sumpters are harnessed and packed;
Then the barons mount up and ride off along the road;
They reach Jericho where they cut many palms; (242)
They shout, loud and clear: "Forward! So help us God!"
The Patriarch mounts a lively mule;
245 As long as daylight shines he accompanies and guides the King.
That night the barons shared lodgings:
Nothing that they asked was refused.
In the morning, at dawn, when they perceive daylight,
The barons mount up again and ride forth along the road;
250 The Patriarch called to Charlemagne:
"Fair Sire, pray give me your leave."
And the Emperor said: "As our Lord God wills!"
They embrace each other, and then they part.
The Emperor is riding on with his doughty barons;

255 Les reliques sunt forz, granz vertuz i fait Deus,
Qu'il ne venent a ewe, n'en partissent les guet,
Ne n'encuntrent aveogle, ne seit reluminet; (257)
Les cuntrez i redrescent et les muz funt parler.

XVII

    Chevalchet l'emperere od sa cumpanie grant, (259)
260 E passent montelés et les puis d'Abilant,
La roche del Guitume e les plaines avant;
Virent Constantinoble, une citez vaillant,
Les clochés et les egles et les punz relusanz. (263)
Destre part la citet, d'une liuee grant, (264)
265 Trovent vergers plantez de pins, de lorers blans; (265)
La rose i est florie, li alburs et l'aiglens. (266)
Vint mile chevalers i troverent seant,
E sunt vestut de pailes et de heremins blans
E de granz peus de martre jok'as pez traïnanz. (269)
270 As eschés et as tables se vunt esbaneant,
E portent lur falcuns et lur osturs asquanz;
E treis mile puceles a orfreis relusant;
Vestues sunt de pailes, et ount cors avenanz, (273)
Et tenent lur amis, si se vunt deportant.
275 Atant es vus Karlun sur un fort mul amblant. (275)
A une part se turnet, si apelet Rollant:
"Ne sai ou est li reis. Ci'st li barnages grant!" (277)
Un chevaler apelet, si li dist en riant:
"Amis, u est li reis? Mult l'ai alet querrant." (279)
280 E icil li ad dist: "Or chevalchet avant: (280)
A cel paile tendut verrez lu rei seant." (281)

---

(257) Nencuntrent a. ki ne s.
(259) li emperere
(263) egles et punz le lusanz
(264) de une liuue g.
(265) pins et de l. beaus
(266) li a. et li glazaus
(269) jokes as p.
(273) ount les cors
(275) Atant est k. sur un mul
(277) reis Ici est li b.
(279) le ai alee q.
(280) Ore
(281) cele paile tendue

255 The relics are powerful and God performs great miracles:
They come to no stream which is not sundered for them to cross,
They do not meet a single blind man whose sight is not restored;
They straighten up the lamed and make the dumb speak.

XVII

The Emperor is riding forth with his large company,
260 And they ride past hillocks and the peaks of Abilant, (260)
The rock of Guitume and the plains beyond; (261)
They see Constantinople, a splendid city,
With its bell-towers, its eagles, and its gleaming domes. (263)
To the right of the city, one good league away,
265 They find gardens planted with pine trees and white laurels,
Places where the roses, the viburnum, and the eglantine are
   in bloom; (266)
There they find twenty thousand knights sitting,
Clad in silk cloth, in white ermine, (268)
And wrapped in long marten furs reaching to their feet;
270 They are enjoying themselves playing chess and backgammon, (270)
And they are bearing their falcons and goshawks. (271)
There are also three thousand maidens wearing glittering
   orphrey robes; (272)
They are clad in silk and are of attractive mien;
They are embracing their lovers and are enjoying themselves.
275 And now comes Charles on a strong ambling mule;
He rides on, a little apart, and calls Roland:
"I do not know where the King is, but this is his magnificent
   assembly!"
He calls to a knight and asks him, smiling:
"My friend, where is the King? Long have I looked for him."
280 And the knight told him: "Continue riding:
You will see the King sitting over there where this silk cloth
   is stretched."

Chevalchet l'emperere, ne se vait atargeant. (282)
Truvat lu rei Hugun a sa carue arant;
Les cunjugles en sunt a or fin relusant, (284
285 Li essués et les röes et li cultres arant.
Il ne vait mie a pet, l'aguilun en sa main, (286)
Mais de chascune part at un fort mul amblant; (287)
Une caiere d'or le sustent en pendant*: (288)
La sist li emperere sur un cuisin vaillant, (289)
290 La plume est d'orïol, la teie escarimant, (290)
As ses pez un escame neelé d'argent blanc, (291)
Sun capel en sun chef; mult par sunt bel li gaunt;
Quatre estaches d'or mier entur lui en estant: (293)
Desus i ad jetet un bon paile grizain. (294)
295 Une verge d'or fin tint li reis en sa main:
Si cundut sun aret tant adreceement (296)
Si fait dreite sa rei cume line que tent. (297)
Atant es vus Carlun sur un fort mul amblant. (298)

XVIII

Li reis tint sa carue pur sun jur espleiter,
300 E vint i Carlemaines tut un antif senter:
Vit le paile tendud et l'or reflambïer. (301)
Lu rei Hugun salue, le Fort, trez volenters. (302)
Li reis regardet Carle; veit le cuntenant fer, (303)

---

(282) li emperere
(284) Les cuningles
(286) le aguilun
(287) part un fort
(288) caiere sus le tent dor suzpendant.
(289) lemperere
(290) de oriol; t. descarimant
(291) escamel n. de argent
(293) estaches entur
(294) Desus ad j.
(296) Si a c.
(297) cum line
(298) A. est vus c. sur un mul
(301) le or
(302) salua
(303) reis Hugun r.

Without delay the Emperor rides forth.
He found King Hugo working the land with his plow;
Its yokes are of fine glittering gold,
285 And also the axles, the wheels, and the plowshare.
The King does not go on foot, his goad in his hand;
Rather he has strong ambling mules, one on each side;
A swinging gold seat supports him:
There sits Emperor Hugo on a sumptuous cushion
290 Whose down is from orioles and its case of silk from Persia;
A footstool inlaid with white silver supports his feet;
His headgear is on his head; his gloves are splendid;
Four posts of pure gold stand around him:
A valuable cloth of silk from Greece is stretched over them.
295 The King is holding a rod of fine gold in his hand:
With such skill is he driving his plow
That he draws a furrow in a straight line.
And now comes Charles on his strong ambling mule.

XVIII

The King was driving his plow to do his day's work,
300 And Charlemagne arrived there following an ancient path:
He saw the stretched silk cloth and the glittering gold;
He greets King Hugo the Strong wholeheartedly.
The King looks at Charles and notices his proud mien,

Les braz gros et quarrez, le cors greile et delget. (304)
305 "Sire, Deu vus garise! De quei me conuset?"
Respont li emperere: "Jo sui de France net;
Jo ai nun Carlemaines, Rolland si est mis nés; (307)
Venc de Jerusalem, si m'en voil retorner;
Vus e vostre barnage voil veer volenters."
310 E dist Hugun* li Forz: "Ben ad set anz e melz
Qu'en ai oï parler estrange soldeers,
Ke issi grant barnages nen ait nul rei suz cel. (312)
Un an vus retendrai, si estre i volez; (313)
Tant vus durrai argent, or et aveir trusset, (314)
315 K'en porterunt Franceis cum en vodrunt charger. (315)
Or dejundrai mes beos pur la vostre amistet." (316)

XIX

Li reis desjunt ses beos et laset sa carue,
E paissent par ces praez, amunt par ces cultures.
Li reis muntet al mul, si s'en vait l'ambleüre. (319)
320 "Sire," dist li reis Carles, "ceste vostre carue,
Tant i at de fin or que jo n'en sai mesure; (321)
Si senz garde remaint, creim qu'ele soit perdue." (322)
E dist Hugun li reis: "De tut ceo n'aez cure: (323)
Unkes nen out larun, tant cum ma terre adure; (324)
325 Set anz i purrat estre, ne serrat remoüe." (325)
Dist Willemes d'Orange: "E, sainz Pere, aiude! (326)
Car la tenise en France, et Bertram si i fusset, (327)

---

(304) braz ad gros
(307) ai a nun
(312) Ke si g. barnages ait nul r.
(313) retenderai
(314) d. or et a. et aveir truss
(315) Tant en p.; cum il en voderunt
(316) Ore
(319) lamblure
(321) jo ne sai
(322) jo creim que ele
(323) tut iceo
(324) ne out
(325) serrat remue
(326) de orenge sainz p.
(327) berteram

His arms strong and well-formed, his body slim and slender. (304)
305 "Sire, may God help you! How do you know me?"
The Emperor answers: "I am from France;
My name is Charlemagne, and my nephew is Roland;
I come from Jerusalem and I want to return;
I would gladly visit with you and your court."
310 And Hugo the Strong said: "At least seven years ago, or more,
I heard foreign soldiers say
That no king on the face of the earth wields as much power as you.
I shall keep you here with me for a year, if you want to stay;
I shall give you so much silver, gold, and so many cases of riches,
315 That your Frenchmen will carry away as much as they will want to load;
And now I am going to unyoke my oxen out of friendship for you."

XIX

The King unyokes his oxen and leaves his plow behind;
They graze in these meadows, also higher up in these cultivated fields.
The King mounts his mule and rides away.
320 "Sire," said King Charles, "this plow of yours
Contains so much fine gold that I cannot estimate it;
If it is left unattended, I am afraid that it might be stolen."
And King Hugo said: "Do not worry about this:
Never has there been any thief in my kingdom, as far as it extends;
325 Seven years could it remain there without being tampered with."
Said William of Orange: "So help us Saint Peter!
If I had it in France, and if Bertrand were there,

A pels et a martels sereit aconseüe, (328)
Li reis brochet le mul, si s'en vait l'ambleüre, (329)
330 E vint sus al paleis, out sa muiller veüe; (330)
Il la fet cunreer, et cele est revestue,
Le paleis et la sale de pailes purtendue. (332)
Atant es vus Carlun od sa grant gent venue. (333)

XX

L'emperere descent defors le marbre blanc; (334)
335 Cez degrez de la sale vint al paleis errant.
Set milie chevalers i troverent seant, (336)
A peliçuns ermins, bliauz escarimant: (337)
As eschés et as tables se vunt esbaneant.
La defors sunt curuz li plusurs et asquanz, (339)
340 Receurent les somiers* et les forz mulz amblanz; (340)
A lur osteus les meinent cunreer gentement. (341)
Charles vit le paleis et la richesce grant:
A or fin sunt les tables, les chaeres, li banc. (343)
Li paleis fu listez d'azur, et avenant (344)
345 Par mult cheres peintures a bestes, a serpenz, (345)
A tutes creatures et a oiseaus volanz. (346)
Li paleis fud voutuz et desure cloanz, (347)
E fu fait par cumpas et seret noblement;
L'estache del miliu neelee d'argent. (349)

---

(328) A peals et a marteals s. escansue
(329) Il brochet; lamblure
(330) E viut; paleis u out
(332) purtendues
(333) A. est vus; grant venue
(334) Li emperere
(336) Set mil ch.
(337) blianz e.
(339) La fors s.
(340) Receurent les destrers et
(341) A les o.
(343) tables et chaeres et li b.
(344) de azur et avernant
(345) Par cheres; bestes et a s.
(346) et oiseaus
(347) fud vout et desur c.
(349) dargent blanc

It would be smashed into pieces with stakes and hammers!"
The King spurs on his mule and rides forth ambling;
330 He comes to his palace where he meets his wife;
He bids her to get ready, and she dresses herself.
The palace and its hall are decorated with hanging silk drapes. (332)
And now comes Charles with many followers.

XX

The Emperor dismounted before reaching the block of white marble, (334)
335 Then walked quickly up the steps into the palace;
There they found seven thousand knights sitting,
Wearing ermine furs and tunics of silk from Persia: (337)
They were enjoying themselves playing chess and backgammon; (338)
Many of them ran down outside
340 To be entrusted with the sumpters and the strong ambling mules,
And they took them to their quarters to be cared for as was fitting.
Charles admired the palace and its great sumptuousness:
The tables, the chairs, and the benches are made of fine gold;
The walls of the palace were decorated with borders of azure, and exquisitely ornamented
345 With costly paintings of beasts, snakes,
And of all kinds of creatures and flying birds;
The palace was vaulted and topped with a tight dome;
It had been built with great care and put up with art;
Its central column is inlaid with silver;

350 Cent colunes i ad tut de marbre en estant: (350)
　　Cascune est a fin or neelee devant,
　　De quivre et de metal tregeté dous enfanz:
　　Cascun tient en sa buche un corn d'ivorie blanc.
　　Si galerne ist de mer, bise ne altre vent
355 Ki ferent al paleis de devers occident, (355)
　　Il le funt turneer et menut et suvent (356)
　　Cumme röe de char qui a tere decent.
　　Cil corn sunent et buglent et tunent ensement (358)
　　Cum taburs u toneires u grant cloches qui pent; (359)
360 Li uns esgardet l'altre ensement en riant (360)
　　Que ço vus fust viarie que tut fussent vivant.
　　Karles vit le paleis et la richece grant;
　　La sue manantise ne priset mie un guant;
　　De sa mullier li membret que manacé out tant. (364)

XXI

365　　"Seignurs," dist Carlemaignes, "mult gent palais ad ci; (365)
　　Tel nen out Alixandre ne li vielz Costantin,
　　Ne n'out Crisans de Rome, qui tanz honurs bastid."
　　E tant cum l'emperere cele parole had dit, (368)
　　Devers les porz de mer uït un vent venir: (369)
370 Vint bruant al palais, d'une part l'acuillit; (370)
　　Cil l'a fait esmuveir et süef et serrit: (371)
　　Altresil fait turner cum arbre de mulin. (372)
　　Celes imagines cornent, l'une a l'altre surrist, (373)
　　Que ceo vus fust viarie que il fussent tuz vis;
375 L'un halt, li altre cler; mult feit bel a oïr:

---

(350) Cent coluns
(355) paleis devers
(356) turner
(358) buglent et sunent e.
(359) Cumme taburs
(360) le altre e. cum en riant
(364) memberet
(365) dist carles
(368) li emperere
(369) de la mer
(370) de une p. le acuillit
(371) suef et et serrit
(372) Altresi le fait
(373) E celes i.

350 One hundred pillars of solid marble stand there:
Each one is inlaid with gold in front,
And flanked with two copper and metal statues of children: (352)
Each child is holding a white ivory horn in his mouth.
Whenever the westerly, the northerly, or any other winds blow from the sea,
355 Winds which strike the palace on its western side,
They make it rotate swiftly without stopping,
Like the wheel of a chariot rushing downhill;
These horns will then resound, bellow, and boom,
Just like drums, or thunder, or a big swinging bell;
360 Then the statues turn to face each other and seem to laugh,
In such a way that you would think that they are alive.
Charles admired the palace and its great sumptuousness,
And he now values his own possessions no more than a glove; (363)
He remembers his wife whom he threatened so much.

XXI

365 "My Lords," said Charlemagne, "what a beautiful palace this one is;
Not Alexander nor old Constantine ever had one like it,
Nor Cressentius of Rome who built so many monuments."
Barely had the Emperor uttered these words,
That he heard a wind blowing from the seaports:
370 It blew in raging against the palace, struck it on one side,
Set it in motion, gently and smoothly:
It made it rotate like the driving shaft of a mill;
The statues are blowing their horns, smiling at one another, (373)
So that you would believe them to be truly alive;
375 One is blowing loud, the other clear; very pleasant are the sounds:

C'est avis, qui l'ascute, qu'il seit en paraïs, (376)
La u li angle chantent et süef et seriz. (377)
Mult fud grant li orages, la neif et li gresilz,
E li vent durs et forz qui tant bruit et fremist. (379)
380 Les fenestres en sunt a cristal mult gentilz, (380)
Tailees et cunfites a brasme utremarin: (381)
Laenz fait tant requeit et süef et serit (382)
Cumme en mai en estet quant soleil esclarcist. (383)
Mult fut gres li orages et hidus et costis*;
385 Karles vit le paleis turneer et fremir: (385)
Il ne sout que ceo fud, ne l'out de luign apris.
Ne pout ester sur pez, sur le marbre s'asist.
Franceis sunt tuz verset, ne se pöent tenir, (388)
E covrirent lur ches et adenz et suvin, (389)
390 E dist li uns a l'altre: "Mal sumes entrepris;
Les portes sunt uvertes, si n'en poüm issir."

XXII

Carles vit le palais menüement turner. (392)
Franceis covrent lur ches, ne l'osent esgarder. (393)
Li reis Hugun li Forz en est avant alez
395 E ad dit a Franceis: "Ne vus descunfortez!"
"Sire," dist Carlemaines, "ne serrat ja mais el?" (396)
E dist Hugun li Forz: "Un petit m'atendet!"
Li vespre aproçat, li orages remest; (398)
Franceis saillent en pez. Tut fut prest li supers;
400 Carlemaines s'asist e sis ruiste barnez, (400)

---

(376) Ceo est a.
(377) chantent suef
(379) bruit et fefreit
(380) cristal gentilz
(381) a braines utre m.
(382) fait itant r.
(383) esclarist
(385) turner
(388) Fraceis sunt
(389) E coverirent
(392) menument
(393) nel osaeut e.
(396) carlemaines serrat
(398) vespere aprocet; remist
(400) Carles

He who hears them believes that he is in paradise,
That place where angels are singing smoothly and sweetly.
The storm was savage with snow and hail,
And the wind which was roaring and striking was harsh and fierce.
380 The windows are made of very fine crystal
Cut and fashioned out of a precious stone from across the sea:
Inside it is as quiet, pleasant, and still
As in the month of May, in summertime, when the sun is shining.
The storm was dreadful and hideous, as it blew in from the sea; (384)
385 Charles could see the palace rotating and shaking:
He did not know what was happening because he had never heard of anything like this;
He was unable to stand on his feet, so he sat down on the marble.
All the Frenchmen are tossed to the floor, they cannot stand up;
Lying on their faces or on their backs, they covered their heads
390 And said to one another: "We surely are in a quandary;
The doors are open, but we cannot get out."

XXII

Charles could see the palace revolving swiftly;
The Frenchmen cover their heads and dare not watch.
Then Hugo the Strong walked forward
395 And said to the Frenchmen: "Do not be worried!"
"Sire," said Charlemagne, "will this ever stop?
And Hugo the Strong answered: "Wait patiently a little!"
As the evening drew near, the storm subsided;
The Frenchmen leapt back on their feet. Dinner was quite ready;
400 Charlemagne and his doughty barons sat down at the table

Li reis Hugun li Forz et sa muiller delez, (401)
Sa fille od le crin bloi qu'ad le vis bel et cler, (402)
E out la char tant blanche cumme flur en ested.
Oliver l'esgardat, si la prist a amer: (404)
405 "Ploüst al rei de glorie, de saincte majestet, (405)
Que la tenise en France, u a Dun* la citet,
Ka jon fereie pus tutes mes voluntez!" (407)
Entre ses denz le dist, qu'hon nel pot escuter. (408)
Nule rein qu'il demandent ne lur fud deveez:
410 Asez unt venesun de cerf et de sengler, (410)
E unt grues et gauntes et poüns enpevrez; (411)
A espandant lur portent le vin et le clarez, (412)
E cantent et vïelent et rotent cil jugler, (413)
E Franceis se desportent par grant nobilitet. (414)

XXIII

415   Cum il ourent manget enz al palais real, (415)
E unt traites les napes li maistre senescal,
Saillent li esquïer en renc de tute parz,
Et si vunt as osteus cunreer lur chevaus. (418)
Li reis Hugun li Forz Carlemaine apelat, (419)
420 Lui et les duzce pers, sis trait a une part;
Le rei tint par la main, en sa cambrel menat, (421)
Voltue, peinte a flurs, a peres de cristal; (422)
Une escarbuncle i luist e cler reflambeat, (423)

---

(401) Hugun l forz
(402) que ad
(404) lesgardet
(405) Plust
(407) Ka jo en freie
(408) que hon
(410) de cerfs
(411) enpeverez
(412) As pandant ur p.
(413) juglur
(414) Franceis se d.; noblitet
(415) Cume il o. enz al p. real manget
(418) Il vuut as o.
(419) carlemain
(421) cambre les m.
(422) Voltrue peint a f. et a p.
(423) cler e r.

With King Hugo the Strong and his wife at his side,
And his daughter, the blond, who had a beautiful fair face, (402)
And whose skin was as white as blossoms in summertime.
Oliver looked at her and felt love for her:
405 "Would the King of Glory in His Holy Majesty,
That she were mine in France, or in the city of Dun; (406)
Then I would have my way!"
He muttered these words between his teeth, so that no one could hear him.
Nothing of what they asked was refused them:
410 They get plenty of venison of deer and wild boar,
And also cranes, wild geese, and peacocks seasoned with pepper; (411)
Wine and clary are gushing forth in abundance; (412)
The minstrels are singing and playing the vielle and the rote, (413)
And the Frenchmen are making merry like noblemen.

XXIII

415 After they had dinner in the royal palace,
And the head seneschals had removed the tablecloths, (416)
The squires rush from all sides, one behind another,
And go to their lodgings to look after their horses. (418)
King Hugo the Strong called to Charlemagne
420 With his Twelve Peers, and he drew them aside;
He held the Emperor by the hand, and he led him to his room
Which was vaulted, decorated by painted flowers and crystals;
A carbuncle was gleaming there, glittering bright; (423)

Confite en une estache del tens le rei Golias;
425 Duze liz i ad dous, de quivre et de metal,
Oreillers de velus e linçous de cendal: (426)
Al menur unt a traire .XX. beos et quatre cars. (427)
Li trezimes en mi est taillez a cumpas: (428)
Li peçul sunt d'argent et l'espunde d'esmal. (429)
430 Li cuverturs fud bons que Maseüz uvrat, (430)
Une fee mult gente qui le rei le dunat: (431)
Melz en vaut li cunreiz del tresor l'Amiral. (432)
Ben deit li reis amer qui li abandunat
E tant ben le servit, et gent le cunreat. (434)

XXIV

435   Franceis sunt en la cambre, si unt veüd les liz;
Casqun des duze pers i ad ja le son pris. (436)
Li reis Hugun li Forz lur fait porter le vin.
Sages fud e membrez, mais plains de maleviz: (438)
En la cambre voltue, suz un perun marbrin (439)
440 Qui fud desuz cavez, si ad un hume mis: (440)
Tute la nuit les gardet par un pertus petit,
Li carbuncles art bien, qu'i pöet hom veïr (442)
Cume en mai en estet quant soleil esclarcist.
Li reis Hugun li Forz a sa muiller en vint. (444)
445 Carlemaines et Franceis se cuchent a leisir: (445)
Des ore gabberunt li cunte et li marchis. (446)
Franceis furent as cambres*, si unt beüz des vins.

---

(426) Oreillers et velus
(427) Al menur a t.
(428) mi etaillez
(429) de argent
(430) cuvertures, uverat
(431) que li reis dunat
(432) la amiral
(434) ben servit
(436) duze peres
(438) membrez plains
(439) cambre desuz un p.
(440) Desuz c. Qui fud *is missing*.
(442) art que bien i p. home veer
(444) muiller e v.
(445) E carlemaines
(446) gabberent

It was inserted in a pillar dating back to the time of King Goliath;
425 There await twelve soft beds made of copper and metal,
With pillows of velvet and sheets of sendal: (426)
Twenty oxen and four carts would be needed to draw the smallest
  of them;
The thirteenth, in the middle, is perfectly fashioned:
Its feet are of silver and its frame of enamel;
430 Its coverlet is finely made, for it was woven by Maseuz,
A very noble fairy who gave it to the King:
The adornment on it is worth more than the Emir's treasure.
The King certainly ought to love her who gave it to him,
Who served him so well, and provided him so generously.

XXIV

435 The Frenchmen were in the room and saw the beds;
Each of the Twelve Peers took his own immediately.
King Hugo the Strong has wine brought to them.
He was wise, cautious, but full of guile:
In the vaulted room, underneath a marble staircase (439)
440 Which was hollow, he hid one of his men:
All night long he watches the Frenchmen through a little hole;
The carbuncle is all aglow so that one can see inside
As well as in May, in summertime, when the sun is shining.
King Hugo the Strong went back to his wife.
445 Charlemagne and his Frenchmen lay down at their ease:
From now on the counts and marquesses will begin to boast.
The Frenchmen were in their room and they drank their
  wines. (447)

XXV

    E dist li un a l'altre: "Veez cum grant bealtet!
Veez cum gent palais e cum forz richetet!
450 Ploüst al rei de glorie, de sainte majestet, (450)
Carlemaines mi sire les oüst recatet (451)
U cunquis par ses armes en bataile champel!"
E lur dist Carlemaines: "Ben dei avant gabber. (453)
Li reis Hugun li Forz nen ad nul bacheler
455 De tute sa mainie, qui tant seit fort membré, (455)
Ait vestu dous haubers et dous halmes fermet, (456)
Si seit sur un destrer curant et sujurnet; (457)
Li reis me prest s'espee al poin d'or adubet, (458)
Si ferrai sur les heaumes u il erent plus chers,
460 Trancherai les haubercs et les heaumes gemmez,
Le feutre avoec la sele del destrer sujurnez; (461)
Le branc ferrai en terre: si jo le lés aler, (462)
Ja nen ert mes rescuz par nul hume charnel (463)
Tresqu'il seit pleine haunste de terre desteret."
465 "Par Deu," ço dist l'eschut, "fort estes et membret!
Refols* fud li reis Hugue quant vus prestat ostel. (466)
Si anuit meis vus oi de folie parler,
Al matin par sun l'albe vus ferai cungeer." (468)

XXVI

    E dist li emperere: "Gabbez, bel neis Rolland!"
470 "Volenters," dist il, "sire, tut al vostre comand! (470)
Dites al rei Hugun quem prest sun olivant; (471)

---

    (450) Plust
    (451) sire le oust
    (453) E dist c.
    (455) sa maine qui
    (456) dous hames fermeet
    (457) curant sujurnet
    (458) prestet sa espee
    (461) feutre od la s.
    (462) branc en t.
    (463) mes receuz par
    (466) hugun
    (468) vus frai c.
    (470) Volonteres sire
    (471) hugun qui il me prestet

XXV

    They said to each other: "Behold this magnificence!
Behold this splendid palace, this vast wealth!
450 Would the King of Glory in His Holy Majesty,
That Charlemagne, my lord, have acquired them,
Or conquered them by force of arms on the battlefield!"
And Charlemagne told them: "I must be the first to boast.
Among all his household, King Hugo does not have a single knight bachelor, (454)
455 However strong and sturdy he might be—
Should he put on two hauberks, two closed helms, (456)
Mount a swift and spirited war-horse,
Should the King lend me his sword with its pommel bedecked with gold, (458)
And should I strike on the helms where they are the most invaluable—
460 Who could prevent me from cutting through the hauberks, the jeweled helms,
And through the horse-cloth and the saddle of the spirited war-horse;
I shall drive the blade deep into the ground: if I let it go,
No man alive will be able to retrieve it
Without digging it out for a full spear's length deep."
465 "My Lord," said the spy, "you are strong and sturdy!
King Hugo was doubly insane when he gave you lodging.
If I still hear you speak such nonsense tonight,
In the morning, at dawn, I shall have you sent away."

XXVI

    And the Emperor said: "Make your boast, fair nephew Roland!"
470 "With pleasure, Sire," said he, "at your command!
Tell King Hugo to lend me his oliphant; (471)

Pus si m'en irrai jo la defors en cel plain: (472)
Tant par ert fort m'aleine, et li venz si bruant, (473)
Qu'en tute la cité, que si est ample et grant, (474)
475 N'i remaindrat ja porte ne postits en astant,
De quivre ne d'acer, tant seit fort ne pesant, (476)
Ke l'un ne ferge a l'altre par le vent si bruant. (477)
Mult ert forz li reis Hugue, s'il se met en avant, (478)
K'il ne perde la barbe, les gernuns en brulant, (479)
480 E les granz peaus de martre qu'ad al col en turnant, (480)
Le peliçun d'ermin del dos en reversant." (481)
"Par Deu," ço dist l'eschut, "ci ad mal gabement! (482)
Que fouls fist li reis Hugue qu'il herbegat tel gent!" (483)

XXVII

"Gabbez, sire Oliver!" dist Rolland li curteis.
485 "Volenters," dist li quens, "mais que Carles l'otrait. (485)
Prenget li reis sa fille, qui tant ad bloi le peil,
En sa cambre nus metet en un lit en requeit;
Si jo ne l'ai anut, tesmoing de lui, cent feiz, (488)
Demain perde la teste, par covent li otrai." (489)
490 "Par Deu," ço dist l'eschut, "vus recrerez anceis! (490)
Grant huntage avez dit; mais quel sacet li reis, (491)
En trestute sa vie mes ne vus amereit!"

---

(472) irrai la fors en c.
(473) ma aleine
(474) Que tute
(476) Ne quivee ne acer
(477) Ke le un; vent qui ert si b.
(478) hugun si il se metet
(479) Ke il ne perde de la barbe
(480) martre qui il ad al c.
(481) de ermin
(482) li eschut
(483) hugun que il
(485) Volenteres; mais carlemaines le o.
(488) anut testimonie de
(489) covent le otrai
(490) li eschut vus vus r.
(491) que il sacet

Then I shall go out over there in that plain:
So powerful will my breath be, and so loud the blast from the horn,
That in all the city, which is so wide and big,
475 No door nor postern of copper or of steel will remain standing, (475)
However strong and heavy they might be:
They will knock against one another because of this roaring wind.
King Hugo will be very strong, if he steps forward
Without having the hairs of his beard burned off,
480 His long marten furs hanging from his neck whirled round, (480)
And his ermine fur cloak worn on his back turned inside out."
"My Lord," said the spy, "this is a bad boast!
King Hugo was mad when he gave lodging to such people!"

XXVII

"Make your boast, Lord Oliver!" said Roland the courteous.
485 "Willingly," answered the count, "with Charles' permission.
Let the King bring his daughter, who is fair-haired,
And let him take both of us to her room and leave us alone in a bed;
If, by her own testimony, I have not taken her a hundred times during the night,
I accept and pledge to be beheaded, tomorrow."
490 "My Lord," said the spy, "you will take back these words before then!
You have spoken words of outrage; but should the King find out,
He will bear against you a lifelong hatred!"

XXVIII

"E vus, sire arcevesque, gaberez vus od nus?"
"Oïl," ço dist Turpin, "par le comant Carlun.
495 Treis des meillurs destrers qui en sa cité sunt (495)
Prenget li reis demain, sin facet faire un curs. (496)
La defors en cel plain, quant melz s'esleserunt,
Jo i vendrai sur destre curant par tel vigur (498)
Que me serrai al terz, et si larrai les deus; (499)
500 E tendrai quatre pumes mult grosses en mun puin,
Sis irrai estruant et getant cuntremunt,
E lerrai les destrers aler a lur bandun:
Se pume m'en escapet ne altre en chet del poin,
Carlemaines mi sire me cret les oilz del frunt!" (504)
505 "Par Deu," ço dist l'escut, "cist gas est bel et bon: (505)
N'i had huntage nul vers lu rei, mun seignur." (506)

XXIX

Dist Willemes d'Orenge: "Seignurs, or gaberai. (507)
Veez cele pelote? Unc greinur ne vi meis: (508)
Entre or fin et argent, gardet cumben i ad!
510 Meinte feiz i sunt mis .XXX. humes en assai:
Ne la porent müer, tant fud pesant li fais. (511)
A une sule main par matin la prendrai,
Puis la larrai aler tres par mi cel palais:
Mais de quarante teises del mur en abatrai." (514)
515 "Par Deu," ço dist l'escut, "ja ne vus en crerai! (515)
Trestut sait fel li reis, s'asaier ne vus fait! (516)
Ainz que seiez calcet, le matin le dirrai."

---

(495) des desmeillurs d. que en sa c.
(496) si en facet
(498) Jo venderai
(499) Qui me; terz si l.
(504) Carlemain; me crevet les
(505) li escut
(506) Vers mun s. lu rei ni had h. nul
(507) de orenge; ore g.
(508) cele grant p.
(511) la poreint m.
(514) abaterai
(515) li escut
(516) reis si asaier

XXVIII

"And you, Lord Archbishop, will you make your boast with us?"
"Yes," answered Turpin, "with Charles' permission.
495 Let the King choose, tomorrow, three of the best war-horses in his city,
And have them race.
When they have reached full speed, out there in the plain,
I shall come from their right, running so rapidly,
That I shall jump over to mount the third, letting the other two run;
500 And I shall hold four very large apples in my hand
That I shall toss and throw high up in the air
While the war-horses are running at full tilt:
If a single apple escapes me, or if I let one drop from my hand,
May Charlemagne my lord claw out my eyes!"
505 "My Lord," said the spy, "this boast is fair and good:
There is no outrage in it against my lord the King."

XXIX

William of Orange then said: "My lords, now I shall make my boast.
Can you see this huge ball over there? Never did I see a bigger one:
Look at the gold and silver that it holds!
510 Many times, up to thirty men have been put to the task:
They could not move it, its weight was so heavy.
Tomorrow morning I shall take it up in a single hand,
And I shall make it roll through the middle of this palace:
Forty lengths of the wall shall I thus knock down."
515 "My Lord," said the spy, "I shall never believe this!
The King is wicked if he does not put you to the test!
I shall tell him tomorrow morning before you have put on your stockings."

XXX

    E dist li emperere: "Or gaberat Ogers, (518)
    Li dux de Denemarche quis put tant traveiller." (519)
520 "Volenters," dist li bers, "tut al vostre cungiet. (520)
    Veez vus cele estache qui le palais sustent, (521)
    Que ui matin veïstes si menut turneer? (522)
    Demain la me verret par vertut embracer:
    Nen ert tant fort l'estache ne l'estucet briser (524)
525 E le palais verser, vers terre trebucer. (525)
    Ki la ert cunseüz, ja garantiz nen ert; (526)
    Mult ert fous li reis Hugue, s'il ne se vait mucer." (527)
    "Par Deu," ço dist l'eschut, "cist hom est enragez! (528)
    Unques Deus ne vus duinst cel gab a cumencer! (529)
530 Que fols fist li reis Hugue qui vus ad herberget!" (530)

XXXI

    E dist li emperere: "Gabez, Naimes li dux!"
    "Volenters," dist li bers. "Tut le peil ai canut: (532)
    Dites al rei Hugun quem prest sun hoberc brun; (533)
    Demain, quant jo l'avrai endosset et vestut, (534)
535 La me verrés escure par force a tel vertuz, (535)
    N'ert tant fort li hobercs d'acer ne blanc ne brun,
    Que n'en cheent les mailles ensement cum festuz." (537)

---

(518) ore g.
(519) qui tant se put traveiller
(520) Volenteres
(521) estache que le p.
(522) matin veistis; turner
(524) Ne ert; le estache ke nel e.
(525) trubucer
(526) ert acunseuz
(527) li reis si il ne
(528) li eschut cist home
(529) gab cumencer
(530) li reis qui
(532) Volenteres
(533) hugun qui il me p.
(534) Demait quant jo laverai
(535) Me verres
(537) cumme festuz

XXX

    And the Emperor said: "Now Ogiers will make his boast,
The Duke of Denmark who could endure so much travail."
520 "Willingly," said the noble knight, "with your permission.
Can you see this column which is supporting the palace
That you saw rotate so swiftly this morning?
Tomorrow you will see me grasp it boldly:
However strong this column may be, it is bound to give way
525 And throw and tumble the palace to the ground;
He who is caught in it will not be saved;
The King will be mad if he does not seek shelter."
"My Lord," said the spy, "this man is insane!
May God never allow you to perform this deed!
530 King Hugo acted like a fool when he gave you lodging!"

XXXI

    And the Emperor said: "Make your boast, Duke Naimes!"
"With pleasure," said the noble knight. "My hair is all hoary,
But tell King Hugo to lend me his burnished hauberk;
Tomorrow, when I have donned it,
535 You will see me bestir myself so hard in it
That, however strong the white or burnished hauberk of steel may be, (536)
Its metal links will break off like as many straws."

"Par Deu," ço dist l'escut, "veilz estes et canuz, (538)
Tut avez le peil blanc; mult avez les ners durs!"

XXXII

540   E dist li empereres: "Gabez, dan Berenger!"
"Volenters," dist li quens, "quant vus le comandez.
Prenget li reis espees de tuz les chevalers,
Facet les enterer trequ'as haltes d'or mer, (543)
Que les pointes en seient cuntremunt vers le cel; (544)
545   En la plus halte tur m'en munterai a pet,
E pus sur les espees m'en larrai derocher:
La verrez brans crussir et espees brisier,
L'un acer depecer a l'altre et entroscher; (548)
Ja ne troverez une qui m'ait en char tuchet, (549)
550   Ne le quir entamet, ne en parfunt plaet."
"Par Deu," ço dist l'eschut, "cist hom est enraget!
Si il cel gab demustre, de fer est u d'acer!" (552)

XXXIII

E dist li empereres: "Sire Bernard, gabez!"
"Volenters," dist li quens, "quant vus le cummandez.
555   Veïstes la grant ewe qui si brut a cel guet? (555)
Demain la ferai tute issir de sun canel, (556)
Aspandre par ces camps, que vus tuz le verrez,
Tuz les celers aemplir qui sunt en la citez, (558)
La gent lu rei Hugun et moillir et guaer, (559)
560   En la plus halte tur lui maïmes munter:
Ja n'en descendrat mais, si l'avrai comandet." (561)
"Par Deu," ço dist l'eschut, "cist hom est enraget!

---

(538) veilz est et
(543) enterer entreque haltes
(544) en seint c.
(548) Lun acer al altre de peces et entre oscher
(549) qui mat en
(552) cel gabs
(555) Veistes cele grant e.
(556) la frai
(558) que sunt
(559) hugun moillir
(561) descendrat sil averai

"My Lord," said the spy, "you are old and hoary,
Your hair is all white, but your muscles are strong!"

XXXII

540 And the Emperor said: "Make your boast, Lord Berenger!"
"Willingly," said the Count, "since you order me.
Let the King take the swords from all his knights,
And have their hilts of pure gold driven into the ground,
So that the blades are pointing up towards the sky;
545 I shall walk up to the top of the tallest tower
And, from up there, I shall throw myself down upon the blades:
There you will see them shattering into pieces, the swords breaking,
And steel splintering and breaking on steel;
But you will not find a single blade which might have cut my flesh,
550 Scratched my skin, or made a deep wound."
"My Lord," said the spy, "this man is insane!
If he performs this boast, he is made of iron or of steel!"

XXXIII

And the Emperor said: "Sir Bernard, make your boast!"
"Gladly," said the Count, "since you order me.
555 Did you see the big river which is rushing loudly at the ford?
Tomorrow I shall make it leave its bed,
Inundate these fields—you will all see it—
And flood all the cellars which are in the city;
I shall have King Hugo's people drench and soak in the water;
560 I shall have the King himself climb up the highest tower:
He will not come down before I tell him."
"My Lord," said the spy, "this man is insane!

Que fols fist li reis Hugue qui vus prestat ostel! (563)
Le matin par sun l'albe serrez tuz cungeez."

XXXIV

565   E dist li quens Bertram: "Or gaberat mis uncles." (565)
"Volenters, par ma fei!" dist Ernalz de Girunde.
"Or prenget li reis Hugue de plum quatre granz sumes, (567)
Sis facet en calderes tutes ensemble fundre,
E prenget une cuve que seit grande et parfunde,
570 Si la facet raser de si que as espondes; (570)
Pus me serrai en mi tresque la basse nune: (571)
Quant li pluns iert tuz pris e rasises les undes,
Cum il ert ben serrez, dunc me verrez escure
E le plum departir et desur mei desrumpre:
575 Nen i remandrat ja pesant une escalunie." (575)
"Ci ad merveillus gab," ceo ad dist li escute; (576)
"Unc de si dure carn n'oï parler sur hume:
De fer est u d'acer, si il cest gab demustret." (578)

XXXV

Ço dist li emperere: "Gabez, sire Aïmer!"
580 "Volenters," dist li quens, "quant vus le comandet. (580)
Uncore ai un capel d'alemande engulet, (581)
D'un grant peisun marage, que fud fait ultre mer:
Quant l'avrai en mun chef vestud et afublet, (582)
Demain quant li reis Hugue serrat a sun deigner,
585 Mangerai sun peisun et bevrai sun claret;
Puis viendrai par detrés, durrai lui un cop tel
Que devant sur sa table le ferai encliner. (587)

---

(563) vus prstat o.
(565) Bertraam
(567) Ore; quatre sumes
(570) raser desque as
(571) basse nuue
(575) remandrat i ja p. un es scalume
(576) li escut
(578) dacer si cest
(580) quant le c.
(581) de almande
(582) p. mage; fait sur (*expunged*) en mer
(587) le frai e.

King Hugo was a fool when he gave you lodging!
In the morning, at daybreak, you will all be expelled."

XXXIV

565   And Count Bertrand said: "Now it is my uncle's turn to make his boast."
"Willingly, by my faith!" said Ernaut of Gironde.
"Now let King Hugo bring four big loads of lead
And have them melted down together in boilers,
Then let him bring a vat, which is big and deep,
570   To have it filled to the brim;
Next I shall sit in the very middle of it until past noon:
When the lead has solidified again and the bubbling has subsided,
And when it has hardened around me, then you will see me bestir myself,
Crack the lead and shake myself free from it:
575   Nothing will be left on me, not even the weight of a shallot." (575)
"This is a wonderful boast," said the spy;
"Never have I heard of a man with such a tough skin:
He must be of iron or steel if he accomplishes this feat."

XXXV

The Emperor said: "Make your boast, Sir Aïmer!"
580   "With pleasure," said the Count, "as you wish.
I still have a hat, decorated with almandines, (581)
Made overseas with the skin of a big sea fish:
When I have put it on my head, (583)
Tomorrow, at the time when King Hugo is having his dinner,
585   I shall eat his fish and drink his clary; (585)
Then I shall come from behind to strike him such a blow
That he will collapse over his table;

La verrez barbes traire et gernuns si peler!"
"Par Deu," ço dist l'escut, "cist hom est enraget! (589)
590 Que fols fist li reis Hugue qui vus presta ostel!"

XXXVI

"Gabez, sire Bertram!" li emperere ad dit. (591)
"Volenters," dist li quens," tut al vostre plaisir.
Treis escuz forz et roiz m'empruntez le matin,
Puis m'en irrai la fors en sum cel pin* antif:
595 Lam les verrez ensemble par tel vertud ferir (595)
E voler cuntremunt; si m'escrïerai, si
Que en quatre liuees envirun le païs (597)
Ne remandrat en bois cerf ne daim a fuïr,
Nule bise salvage ne chevrol ne gupil." (599)
600 "Par Deu," ço dist l'escut, "mal gabement ad ci! (600)
Quant le savrat li reis, grains en ert et maris." (601)

XXXVII

"Gabez, sire Gerin!" dist l'emperere Carles. (602)
"Volenters," dist li quens. "Demain, veant les altres,
Un esped fort et roist m'aportez en la place; (604)
605 Que grant seit et pesant: uns vilains i ait carges; (605)
La haunste de pomer, de fer i ait une alne; (606)
En sumet cele tur, sur cel piler de marbre,
Me culchez dous deners, que li uns seit sur l'altre;
Puis m'en istrai ensus d'une liuee large: (609)
610 Si me verrez lancer, si vus en prenez garde, (610)

---

(589) li escut
(591) Bertraram
(595) La les me verrez
(597) liues
(599) cheverol
(600) li escut
(601) le saverat li reis hugun grains ert
(602) sire genin
(604) espeed
(605) i at carges
(606) Li haunste; un alne
(609) Puis mensterrai e. de une liue l.
(610) vus empernez g.

Then, as a result, you will see beards being tugged and mustaches being torn out!"
"My Lord," said the spy, "this man is mad!
590 King Hugo was out of his mind when he gave you lodging!"

XXXVI

"Make your boast, Sir Bertrand!" the Emperor said.
"Willingly," said the Count, "at your pleasure.
Get me, tomorrow morning, three strong and sturdy shields;
Then I shall go out there to climb up to the top of this ancient pine tree:
595 There you will see me knocking them one against the other vigorously (595)
And tossing them up high in the air; then I shall utter such loud cries
That within a four league radius about the countryside,
No stag, deer, wild doe, roebuck, nor fox
Will remain long in the woods before taking to flight."
600 "My Lord," said the spy, "this is a bad boast!
When the King finds out, he will be angry and sorry."

XXXVII

"Make your boast, Sir Gerin!" Emperor Charles said.
"Gladly," said the Count; "tomorrow, before all the others,
Bring me here a strong and stout spear;
605 Select it long and heavy, weighty for a peasant,
With a shaft of apple-wood and a head one ell long. (606)
At the top of this tower, on this pillar of marble,
Place two pennies, one on top of the other;
Then I shall move a good league away:
610 If you are paying attention, you will see me throw my spear

Tresqu'al piet de la tur, l'un des deners abatre (611)
Si süef et serid, ja nes muvrat li altre; (612)
Puis serrai si legers et ignals et aates, (613)
Que m'en vendrai curant par mi l'us de la sale (614)
615 E reprendrai l'espet ainz qu'a tere s'abaiset." (615)
"Par Deu," ço dist l'escut, "cist gab valt .III. des altres:
Vers mun seignur lu rei n'i ad gens de huntage."

XXXVIII

Quant li cunte unt gabet, si s'en sunt endormit.
Li eschut ist de cambre, qui trestut ad oït,
620 Vint a l'us de la cambre u li reis Hugue gist;
Entreuvert l'ad troved, sin est venuz al lit. (621)
L'empere le vit, hastivement li dist: (622)
"Di, va! que funt Franceis et Karles al fer vis? (623)
Oïstes les parler s'il remaindrunt a mi?" (624)
625 "Par Deu!" ço dist l'escut, "unc ne lur en suvint; (625)
Asez vus unt anut gabet et ascarnit."
Tuz les gas li cuntat, quancque il en oïd. (627)
Quant l'entent li reis Hugue, grains en fud et mariz.

XXXIX

"Par ma fei," dist li reis, "Carles ad feit folie (629)
630 Quant il gaba de moi par si grant legerie:
Herberjai les ersair en mes cambres* perines.
Si ne sunt aampli li gab cum il les distrent, (632)

---

(611) tur lu un deners
(612) et tercid ja nesmuera li a.
(613) et ates
(614) le us de la
(615) E repundrai les peet ainz
(621) troved si sen est v.
(622) Li emperere
(623) que sunt F.; Karles od le fer
(624) Ois les p.; remaindrumm
(625) li escut
(627) Tuz les cuntat
(629) Perar ma f.
(632) gab si cum

As far as the foot of the tower, and knock off one of the pennies
So skillfully that the other one will not budge;
Then I shall be so fleet-footed, so swift, and so agile
That I shall come running through the doorway of the hall
615 To catch the spear before it strikes the ground."
"My Lord," said the spy, "this boast is worth three of the others:
It does not at all slight the King!"

XXXVIII

When the counts finished making their boasts, they fell asleep.
The spy leaves the room, for he has heard everything;
620 He came to the door of the room where King Hugo was lying;
He found it ajar, so he went to the bed.
The Emperor saw him and asked briskly:
"Say! What are the Frenchmen and Charles with the proud face doing?
Did you hear them say whether they are going to stay with me?"
625 "My Lord," said the spy, "they did not even think of that;
They have greatly mocked and insulted you this night."
He told him all about the boasts he had heard.
When King Hugo heard him, he became angry and sorry.

XXXIX

"By my faith," said the King, "Charles acted madly
630 When he made fun of me so foolishly:
I gave them lodging last night in my rooms of stone; (631)
If they do not carry out their boasts, as they made them,

Trancherai lur les testes od m'aspee furbie!"
E mandet de ses humes en avant de cent mile. (634)
635 Il lur ad cumandet qu'aient brunies vesties (635)
E capes afublez, ceint espees brunies; (636)
Il entrent al palais et entur lui s'asistrent. (637)
Karles vint del muster quant la messe fu dite, (638)
Il et li duze per, les feres cumpainies;
640 Devant vait l'emperere, car il est li plus riches, (640)
E portet en sa main un ramisel d'olive. (641)
Li reis Hugue le vit, de luinz le cuntraliet:
"Carles, pur quei gabastes de moi et escarnistes? (643)
Ersair vus herberjai en mes cambres perines:
645 Nel dusez ja penser par si grant legerie; (645)
S'or ne sunt aampli li gab que vus deïstes, (646)
Trancherai vus les testes od m'aspee furbie."
Quant l'entent l'emperere, si se creinst de sa vie, (648)
E regardet Franceis, les feres compaignies: (649)
650 "Del vin et del claret fumes ersair tuz ivres;
Jo quid que li reis out en sa cambre s'espie." (651)

XL

"Sire," dist Carlemaines, "ersair nus hebergastes;
Del vin et del claret asez nus en donastes; (653)
Si'st tel custume en France, a Paris et a Cartres, (654)
655 Quant Franceis sunt culchiez, que se giuent et gabent, (655)
E si dient ambure et saver et folage.

---

(634) de cennt m.
(635) qu'aient vestu brunies
(636) afublez et ceintes e. burnies
(637) palais entur
(638) vint de m.
(640) li emperere
(641) de olive
(643) escarnites
(645) penser pa si g.
(646) Si ore ne
(648) creinst de sai. Vie *is missing*.
(649) compaigines
(651) quid qui li r.
(653) et de el asez nus
(654) Si est tel
(655) se guiunt

I shall cut off their heads with my furbished sword!"
And he summons more than one hundred thousand of his men;
635 He ordered them to don their byrnies, (635)
Their cloaks, and to gird on their burnished swords;
They entered the palace and sat around him.
Charles came back from church after the mass was finished,
He and his Twelve Peers, with his fierce companions;
640 The Emperor marches ahead, for he is the mightiest,
And he has an olive branch in his hand.
King Hugo has seen him, and he calls to him from a distance:
"Charles, why did you make boasts about me and insult me?
Last night I gave you lodging in my rooms of stone:
645 Never should such a foolish thought have entered your mind;
Now if the boasts that you made are not carried out,
I shall cut off your heads with my furbished sword."
When the Emperor hears this, he fears for his life
And looks at his Frenchmen, at his fierce companions:
650 "Yesterday evening we were all drunk from the wine and the clary;
I do believe that the King had his spy in his room."

XL

"Sire," said Charlemagne, "yesterday evening you gave us lodging;
You gave us plenty of wine and clary;
Such is the custom in France, in Paris, and at Chartres,
655 That Frenchmen, when they have gone to bed, tease each other and make boasts,
And engage in both wise and foolish talk.

Or me lesez parler a mun ruiste barnage: (657)
Si vus en respondrai certes par guionage." (658)
"A fei," ço dist li reis, "trop i out grant huntage* . . .
660 Par ma fei," ço dist Hugue, "et par ma blanche barbe,
Quant de mei partirez, ne gaberet mais altre!" (661)

XLI

Carlemaines s'en turnet, li .XII. per od lui, (662)
E vunt en un cunseil desuz un arc volsud. (663)
"Seignurs," dist l'emperere, "mal nus est avenud:
665 Del vin et del claret tant eümes beüd, (665)
E desimes tel chose, que estre ne deüst." (666)
E ad fait les reliques aporter devant lui;
A ureisuns se getent, s'unt lur culpes batud, (668)
E prïent Deu del cel et la sue vertud,
670 Del rei Hugun le Fort qu'il les garisset ui, (670)
Que encuntre lur est si forment irascud. (671)
Atant es vus un angele que Deus i aparut, (672)
E vint a Carlemaine, si l'ad releved sus: (673)
"Carles, ne t'esmaer, ço te mandet Jhesus; (674)
675 Des gas qu'ersair desistes, grande folie fud: (675)
Ne gabez ja mes hume, te cumandet Christus. (676)
Va, si fas cumencer, ja nen i faldrat uns!" (677)
L'emperere l'entent: leez et joiant fud. (678)

---

(657) Ore
(658) responderai volenters par vionage
(661) partirez ja ne g.
(662) turnet et li .XII. p.
(663) arc usud
(665) De vin
(666) tele chose; ne dust
(668) getent si unt
(670) fort que il les
(671) est forment
(672) Atant ast vus un a. qui deus
(673) E unt a c.
(674) Carlemaines ne
(675) desistes grant f.
(676) Ne gabez mes h. ço te c.
(677) ja nen f.
(678) joiant en fud

Now let me address my valiant barons:
Then I shall gladly hold myself responsible for them, on my word."
"By my faith," said the King, "too grievous was the insult . . ."
660 "By my faith," said Hugo, "and by my hoary beard,
When you leave me, you will never make fun of anyone else!"

XLI

Charlemagne turns away and leaves with his Twelve Peers,
And they go to take counsel beneath an arch.
"My lords," said the Emperor, "we are in a predicament:
665 We had so much of the wine and clary,
That we said such things which we ought not to have said."
Then he had the relics brought before him;
They throw themselves to their knees, they beat their breasts,
And pray to the God of heaven and to his power
670 To save them, on that day, from King Hugo the Strong,
Who is so angry at them.
At that time there came an angel sent by God;
He went to Charlemagne and raised him up:
"Charles, fear not, so Jesus tells you;
675 The boasts that you made last night were great madness:
Never again make fun of any man, thus Christ enjoins you.
Go ahead, start carrying them out; not a single one will fail!"
The Emperor hears him well: he is happy and joyful.

XLII

Carlemaines de France, il fud leved en pez (679)
680　E out drescé sa main, en croiz seigna sun chef,
E ad dit a Franceis: "Pas ne vus esmaez!
Devant lu rei Hugun, al palais en venez."

XLIII

"Sire," dist Carlemaines, "ne puis lesser nel die: (683)
Erseir nus herberjastes en vus cambres perines;
685　Del vin et del claret li asquanz furent ivres. (685)
Quant de nus vus turnastes, grant outrage feïstes: (686)
En la cambre leisastes oveoc nus vostre espie.
Nus savun itel terre u custume est asise, (688)
Si vus l'eüsez fait, i eüst felunie. (689)
690　Nus les aamplirun, ne puet remaner mie:
Ki en avrez çoisit, cil comencerat primes." (691)
E dist Hugue le Fort—ne l'ad mesçoisi mie—:
"Ci astat Oliver, qui dist si grant folie
Qu'en une sule nuit avreit cent feiz ma fille. (694)
695　Fel seie en tutes curz si jo ne li delivre! (695)
Si ne li abandun, dunc ne me pris jo mie;
Mais faille une feiz par sa recreantise, (697)
Trancherai lui la teste a m'aspee furbie:
Il et li duze per sunt livred a martirie!" (699)
700　Carlemaines s'en rist, que en Deu s'en afied, (700)
E dist a l'altre mot: "Ja mar l'en larrez quite!" (701)
Tute jur se deportent, giuent et esbanient;
Nule ren qu'il demandent ne lur atarge mie, (703)

---

(679) en peez
(683) ne puus lesser
(685) furent iveres
(686) de nus turnastes
(688) Nus savunn itele t.
(689) i ust f.
(691) en avez c.　icil c.
(694) **Que une s.**; avereit
(695) jo li nel delivre
(697) une sule feiz
(699) et le duze p.
(700) sen afiod
(701) len larred.　Quite *is missing.*
(703) ren que il d.

XLII

　　　Charlemagne of France stood up;
680　He raised his hand and he crossed himself;
　　　Then he said to his Frenchmen: "Do not be afraid!
　　　Come to the palace, before King Hugo."

XLIII

　　　"Sire," said Charlemagne, "I cannot but tell you:
　　　Yesterday evening you gave us lodging in your rooms of stone,
685　And some of us got drunk from the wine and the clary.
　　　When you turned away and left, you committed a great outrage against us:
　　　You left your spy behind in your room with us.
　　　We know a country where the custom is such that,
　　　If you had done this, it would have been regarded as a crime;
690　Yet we shall carry out our boasts; it cannot be otherwise:
　　　Whomever you will have chosen will begin first."
　　　And Hugo the Strong said—he did not make a bad choice—:
　　　"Here is Oliver who said so outrageously
　　　That he would take my daughter a hundred times in a single night.
695　I shall be regarded as wicked in all courts if I do not give her over to him!
　　　If I do not give her up to him, I do not have any self-respect;
　　　But, should he fail only once, out of exhaustion,
　　　Then I shall cut off his head with my furbished sword:
　　　He and the Twelve Peers are certain to suffer martyrdom!"
700　Charlemagne laughs at this, because he has faith in God,
　　　And he adds: "It would be wrong to exempt him!"
　　　All day long the Frenchmen make merry, playing and enjoying themselves;
　　　Everything that they need is brought to them on the spot,

Tresqu'il vint a la nuit, que tut est aserie.
705 Li reis fait en sa cambre acunduire sa fille; (705)
Purtendue est trestute de pailles, de curtines. (706)
Ele out la carn tant blanche cume flur d'albespine. (707)
Oliver i entrat, si començat a rire.
Quant le vit la pucele, mult est aspoürie;
710 Purquant si fud curteise, gente parole ad dite:
"Sire, eissistes de France pur nus, femmes, ocire?" (711)
E respund Oliver: "Ne dutez, bele amie:
Si crere me volez, tute en serrez garie."

XLIV

Oliver gist el lit lez la fille le rei;
715 Devers sei l'a turnet, si la beisat .III. feiz. (715)
Icele fud ben cointe, et il dist que curteis: (716)
"Dame, mult estes bele, s'estes fille de rei; (717)
Pureoc, si dis mun gab, ja mar vus en crendrez;
De vus mes volentez aamplir quier a veir*!" (719)
720 "Sire," dist la pucele, "aiez merci de mei:
Jamés ne serrai lee se vus me huniset!"
"Bele," dist Oliver, "al vostre cumant seit,
Mais que de men cuvent m'aquitiez vers lu rei; (723)
De vus ferai ma drue, ja ne quer altre aveir." (724)
725 Cele fud ben curteise, si l'en plevit sa fei.
Li quens ne li fist mes, la nuit, que .XXX. feiz*. (726)
Al matin par sum l'albe i est venuz li reis
E apelat sa fille, si li dist en requeit:
Dites mei, bele fille, ad le vus fait .C. feiz?"
730 Icele li respunt: "Oïl, bel sire reis!" (730)

---

(705) cambre cunduire sa f.
(706) pailles et de c.
(707) cum flur en este
(711) Sire eissistis de
(715) Devers se la t.
(716) Ele fud
(717) bele car estes f.
(719) aamplir ço ne quier aveir
(723) Mais men cuvent que maquitet v.
(724) vus frai
(726) fist la nuit mes que
(730) Cele li r. oil sire

Until night came when all is still.
705 Then the King has his daughter accompanied to her room;
It is hung with silk draperies and curtains. (706)
Her skin was as white as a hawthorn flower. (707)
Oliver walked in and started to laugh;
When the maiden saw him, she became quite frightened;
710 Yet she knew how to behave herself, and she uttered courteous words:
"My Lord, is it to slaughter us, women, that you left France?"
And Oliver answers: "Do not be afraid, fair friend:
If you are willing to trust me, you will be safe."

XLIV

Now Oliver is in bed next to the King's daughter.
715 He turned her around to him and gave her three kisses.
She was well-bred, and he spoke like a nobleman:
"My Lady, you are beautiful and you are the daughter of a king;
That is why, even though I made this boast, you should not be afraid;
I truly wish that you allow me to carry it out." (719)
720 "My Lord," said the maiden, "have mercy on me:
Never shall I be happy again if you bring dishonor on me!"
"Fair Lady," said Oliver, "I shall do as you wish,
Provided you help me to be released by the King from my boast;
I want you to become my love; I do not wish anyone else." (724)
725 She was very noble and she pledged her faith.
That night, the Count did not take her more than thirty times. (726)
In the morning, at dawn, the King walked in the room,
Called his daughter aside and asked her:
"Tell me, my fair daughter, did he take you a hundred times?"
730 She answers him: "Indeed, fair Sire!"

Ne fait a demander s'irascud fu li reis: (731)
Vint errant al palais u Carles se seeit: (732)
"Li primers est gariz. Encantere est, ço crei! (733)
Or voil saveir des altres si mençunge est u veir." (734)

XLV

735 Dolenz fud li reis Hugue del gab qu'est aampliz, (735)
E dist a Carlemaine: "Li primers est gariz, (736)
E voil saveir des altres s'il ferunt altresi."
"Cil recomencerat ki en avrez çoisit." (738)
Veez ici Willeme, filz le cunte Ameri: (739)
740 Or prenget la pelote ke en la cambre gist; (740)
Si issi ne la getet, cum il erseir le dist,
Trancherai lui la teste a mun brant acerin:
Il et li duze pers sunt venuz a lur fin."

XLVI

Or veit li quens Guillames que li gas fud sur lui; (744)
745 Dunc desfublet ses paus dunt li bevres fud bruns; (745)
Par les neiles* de paile il les ad getet jus. (746)
Vint errant en la cambre u la pelote fud,
A une main la levet, si la trait par vertud,
Si la lessat aler, que trestut l'unt veüd:
750 Mais de quarante teises ad del mur abatud!
Ne fu mie par force, mes par la Deu vertud, (751)
Pur amur Carlemaine chis i out acunduit.

---

(731) si irascud
(732) E vint al p. u carlemaines seait
(733) encanteres
(734) Ore
(735) li reis del g. que est
(736) dist carlemaine
(738) Cil comencerat ki en avez c.
(739) La veez ci Willeme
(740) Ore
(744) Ore; qui li gas
(745) li beveris f.
(746) paile les ad g.
(751) par deu v.

Needless to ask whether the King was angry:
He went immediately to the palace where Charles was sitting:
"The first one is safe; I believe he is a wizard!
Now I want to find out whether the others told a lie or spoke the truth."

XLV

735   King Hugo was distressed that the boast was performed.
He told Charlemagne: "The first one is safe,
But I want to find out whether the others will do as well."
"It will be up to whomever you will have chosen."
"Here is William, Count Aïmeri's son:
740 Now let him take the ball which is in the room;
If he does not throw it here, as he said he would yesterday evening,
I shall cut off his head with my steel sword:
He and the Twelve Peers have come to their end."

XLVI

Now Count William can see that it is up to him to carry out his boast;
745 Therefore he takes off his furs of brown beaver;
By their silk aglets he hurls them to the ground.
He hurried to the room where the ball was,
Lifted it with one hand, cast it with strength,
And he let it roll in such a way—in full sight of all—
750 That it knocked down forty lengths of the wall!
This was not achieved by his sheer strength,
     but by the power of God,
For love of Charlemagne who had led them there.

XLVII

    Dolenz fud li reis Hugue de sun palais ki fend*. (753)
Si ad dit a ses humes: "Ci ad mal gabement: (754)
755 Par la fei que vus dei, nen est ne bel ne gent; (755)
Ces sunt ancanteür qui sunt entrez ceenz: (756)
Volent tenir ma tere et tuz mes casemenz.
Or voil saver des altres si ferunt ensement; (758)
Mais si un sul en fault, par Deu omnipotent, (759)
760 Demain les ferai pendre en sum cel pin* al vent, (760)
A unes forz estaches: nen avrunt raement!" (761)

XLVIII

    "Sire," dist Carlemaines, "volez en mes des gas?
Ki en avrez çoisit, cil recumencerat." (763)
E dist Hugue li Forz: "Veez ici Bernard, (764)
765 Filz le cunte Aimeri, ki de ço se vantat, (765)
Que icele grant ewe qui si brut a cel val, (766)
Qu'il la fereit eisir tute de sun canal, (767)
Entrer en la citet, curre de tutes parz,
Mei maïmes munter en mun plus halt palais, (769)
770 Que n'en purrai decendre tresqu'il cumanderat."

XLIX

    Or set li quens Bernard lui estut cumencer, (771)
E dist a Carlemaine: "Damnedeu en pr̈iez!"

---

(753) ki fud fenduz
(754) humes mal gabement ad ci
(755) que si dei nen est bel ne gentilz
(756) ancantur
(758) Ore
(759) si un en f.
(760) les frai p.
(761) nen averunt raidement
(763) en avez c.
(764) veez ci b.
(765) cunte aimer
(766) Que ile grant e. que brut
(767) la freit e.
(769) Mai mames m.
(771) Ore

XLVII

    King Hugo was grieved because his palace was in ruins.
He said to his men: "This is a bad deed:
755 By the faith that I owe you, this to me is not fair or worthy;
These are wizards who have entered here:
They want to lay hands on my kingdom and on all my fiefs.
Now I want to find out whether the others will do as well;
But if a single one fails, by God the Almighty,
760 Tomorrow I shall have them hanged at the top of this pine tree, in the wind, (760)
By strong bonds: they will receive no pardon!"

XLVIII

    "Sire," said Charlemagne, "do you wish to have more feats?
Whomever you will have chosen will carry on."
And Hugo the Strong said: "Here is Bernard,
765 Count Aïmeri's son, who boasted
That he would make this great river, which is rushing down that valley,
Entirely leave its bed,
Flood the city and spread all over;
That I myself would have to climb up to the top of my highest palace,
770 And that I could not come down until being ordered by him."

XLIX

    Now Count Bernard knows that he has to begin,
And he told Charlemagne: "Pray to the Lord God!"

Il vent curant a l'ewe, si ad les guez seignez:
Deus i fist tel miracle, li glorius del cel, (774)
775 Que tute la grant ewe fait isir de sun bied,
Aspandre par les camps, que tuz le virent ben, (776)
Entrer en la citez et emplir les celers,
La gent lu rei Hugun et moiller et guaer; (778)
En la plus halte tur li reis s'en fuid a ped.
780 Desur un pin* antif est Carles al vis fer,
Il et li duze pers, le barun chevaler,
Et prient Dampnedeu que d'eauls ait grant pited. (782)

L

Desur un pin antif est li reis Carlemaines, (783)
Il et li duze per et les gentes cumpaines; (784)
785 Oït lu rei Hugun sus en la tur deplaindre:
Sun tresor li durat, sil cundurat en France
E devendrat ses homes, de lui tendrat sun regne.
Quant l'entend l'empereere, pitet en a mult grande (788)
—Envers humilitet se deit eom ben enfraindre—
790 E priet a Jhesu que cele ewe remaignet.
Deus i fist grant vertut pur amur Carlemaigne:
L'eve ist de la citet, si s'en vait par les plaines,
Rentret en sun canal, les rives en sunt pleines. (793)
Des or put ben li reis jus de la tur decendre, (794)
795 E vent a Carlemaine desuz l'umbre d'une ente: (795)
"A feiz, dreiz empereere, jo sai ke Deus vus aime;
Tis hom voil devenir, de tei tendrai mun regne;
Mun tresor te durrai, si l'amenrai en France." (798)
"Volez en mes des gas, sire?" dist Carlemaine.
800 E dist Hugue li Forz: "Ne de ceste semaine!
Si tuz sunt aampli, ja n'ert jur ke nem plaigne!" (801)

---

(774) fist miracles
(776) Aspandere les c.
(778) gent lui rei h.
(782) Prient d. qui d'eauls ait pited
(783) est carlemaines
(784) per le gentes
(788) leperere
(793) Reentret en
(794) Des put b.
(795) de une ente
(798) si frai amener en f.
(801) ja ne ert jur ke ne me p.

He ran up to the river and made the sign of the cross over the fords:
God, in His celestial Glory performed such a miracle
775 That he had the whole river leave its bed,
Spread over the fields—in full sight of all—
Enter the city and flood the cellars,
And drench and soak King Hugo's people;
The King flees on foot to his highest tower.
780 Charles with the proud face is high up in an ancient pine tree, (780)
He and his Twelve Peers, the valiant knights,
And they pray to the Lord God to have mercy on them.

L

King Charlemagne is high up in an ancient pine tree,
He and his Twelve Peers, and his worthy companions;
785 He heard King Hugo lamenting on top of his tower:
The King will give him his treasure and will carry it to France;
He will become his liegeman; from him will he hold his kingdom.
When the Emperor hears this, he is filled with great mercy—
Faced with humility, one should break off hostilities—,
790 And he prays to Jesus to make the river recede.
God performed a great miracle for love of Charlemagne:
The water recedes from the city, flowing back over the plains,
Returning to its bed and filling it to the banks.
Now the King can indeed climb down from his tower;
795 He goes to Charlemagne, under the shade of a fruit tree:
"By my faith, worthy Emperor, I do know that God loves you;
I want to become your liegeman; from you shall I hold my kingdom;
I shall give you my treasure, and I shall carry it to France."
"Do you want any more feats, Sire?" said Charlemagne.
800 And Hugo the Strong answered: "Not this week!
If they are all carried out, I shall grieve over it every day of my life!"

LI

"Sire," dist Carlemaines al rei Hugun le Fort,
"Ore estes vus mis heoms, veant trestuz les voz; (803)
Hui devums faire feste, barnage et grant deport, (804)
805 E porterum ensemble les corunes a or.
Pur la vostre amistet prest sui la meie en port." (806)
"E jo, sire, la meie," dist Hugue, "al vostre los: (807)
Ferum processiun la dedenz cel enclos." (808)
Karlemaines portat la grant corone a or, (809)
810 Li reis Hugue la sue, plus basement un poi:
Karlemaines fud graindre de plein ped et .III. pouz. (811)
Franceis les esgarderent, n'i out un n'en parolt: (812)
"Ma dame la reïne folie dist et tord; (813)
Mult par est Karles ber pur demener esforz: (814)
815 Ja ne vendrum en terre nostre ne seit li los." (815)

LII

Karles portet corune dedenz Costentinoble, (816)
Li reis Hugue la sue plus bassement uncore.
E Franceis les esgardent, li plusur en parolent: (818)
"Ma dame la reïne, ele dist mult que fole,
820 Qu'ele* preisat barnet si ben cume le nostre!" (820)
Si funt processiun la dedenz cel encloistre; (821)
La femme lu rei Hugue*, ke sa corune en portet,
Par la main tent sa fille, ke ad la crine bloie; (823)

---

(803) veant tuz les v.
(804) devums vus faire
(806) la mei en p.
(807) la mei dist
(808) Si ferum; cel clos
(809) Karlemaines portet
(811) fud graidre plein p.
(812) les esgardent
(813) la reine dist folie et t.
(814) est Karlemaines b.
(815) terre nortre ne
(816) Karlemaines p.
(818) franceis les e.
(820) Que preisat; cum la nostre
(821) Si ferunt p.; dedenz en cel e.
(823) le crin b.

LI

"Sire," said Charlemagne to King Hugo the Strong,
"You have now become my liegeman, in the presence of all your people;
Today we must celebrate, feast and have great entertainment;
805　And we shall wear our gold crowns side by side.
I am ready to wear mine out of friendship for you."
"And I, mine," said Hugo, "in your honor:
We shall have a procession in there, in this cloister."
Charlemagne wore his great crown of gold,
810　King Hugo his, a little lower:
Charlemagne was one full foot and three inches taller.
The Frenchmen watched them; not a single one refrained from saying:
"My Lady the Queen spoke nonsense and wrong;
Charles is surely a warrior to lead great forces:
815　We shall enter no land where fame will not be ours."

LII

Charles is wearing his crown in Constantinople;
King Hugo his, yet a little lower.
The Frenchmen are watching them; many of them are making comments:
"My Lady the Queen spoke as a mad woman,
820　When she judged that any worthiness could match ours!"
They are walking in procession in there, in that cloister.
King Hugo's spouse, who is wearing her crown,
Is holding by the hand her fair-haired daughter.

Hu que veit Oliver, volenters i parolet, (824)
825 Fait lui contenant gent e amisté li portet: (825)
Volenters le baisast, mais pur sun pere n'oset. (826)
Il entrent al muster, cum issent de l'encloistre. (827)
L'arcevesque Turpin, ki maistre fud des ordres, (828)
Il lur cantat la messe, et li barnet i ofret;
830 Puis venent al palais demeinant grant baldorie. (830)

LIII

Franceis sunt al palais, tuz fud prest li digners;
Les tables sunt drecees, et sunt alez manger. (832)
Nule ren qu'il demandent ne lur fud demured:
Asez unt veneisun de cerf et de sengler,
835 E unt grues et gantes et poüns enpevrez; (835)
A espandant lur portent le vin et le claret, (836)
E cantent et vïelent et rotent cil geugler.
Li reis Hugue li Forz ad Carlun apeled: (838)
"Trestuz mes granz tresor vus seit abandunez: (839)
840 Tant en prengent Franceis cum en voldrunt porter!" (840)
E dist li emperere: "Tut ço lasset ester! (841)
Ja n'en prendrunt del vostre un dener muneed: (842)
Ja unt il tant del mon qu'il nel pöent porter!
Le cunget nus dunet, nus en cuvent aler!" (844)
845 E dist Hugue li Forz: "Jo nel vus os veer."
—Les mulz e les sumers lur tint l'em as degrez—. (846)
E dist li emperere: "Si cum vus cumandez." (847)

---

(824) i parolt
(825) lui contenance gente amiste
(826) pere nen oset
(827) cum il issent
(828) Li ercevasque
(830) palais si d.
(832) Les tabeles furent d.
(835) enpeverez
(836) Espandant lur
(838) ad carlemaine a.
(839) vus seint a.
(840) cum il en volderunt
(841) tut ico l.
(842) nen prendrai del
(844) Mes des ore le cunget nus en dunet cuvent aler
(846) mulz lur tint lem as marbrins degreez
(847) dist leperere

As soon as the blonde sees Oliver, she is glad to speak to him:
825 She shows him a welcoming mien and displays her affection:
She would gladly kiss him, but she does not dare because of her father.
After coming out of the cloister they enter the church.
Archbishop Turpin, who was at the head of the clergy,
Sang the mass for them, and the barons made their offerings;
830 Then they came to the palace, showing great jubilation.

LIII

The Frenchmen are in the palace; dinner was quite ready;
The tables were set up, and they went to eat;
Nothing for which they asked was refused:
They get venison of deer and boar to satiation,
835 And cranes, wild geese, and peacocks seasoned with pepper; (835)
Wine and clary are gushing forth in abundance;
Minstrels are singing and playing the vielle and the rote. (837)
King Hugo the Strong called to Charles:
"I give up to you all my vast treasure:
840 May your Frenchmen take away as much as they wish to carry!"
And the Emperor said: "Forget that!
They will never take away a single penny from your wealth:
They have already so much from mine that they cannot carry it!
Pray give us leave: we must go!"
845 And Hugo the Strong said: "I do not dare forbid you."
The mules and sumpters were kept ready by the stairs.
And the Emperor said: "As you command."

Vunt sei entrebaiser, a Deu sunt cumandez.

LIV

    Quant Franceis unt manget, des ore s'en irrunt.
850 Les mulz et les sumers lur tint om as peruns;
    Si sunt muntez Franceis qui a joie s'en vunt. (851)
    La fille lu rei Hugue* i curt tut a bandun
    La u veit Oliver, sil prent par sun gerun:
    "A vus ai jo turnet m'amistet et m'amur; (854)
855 Que m'en portez en France, si m'en irrai od vus!" (855)
    "Bele," dist Oliver, "m'amur vus abandun:
    Jo m'en irrai en France od mun seignur Carlun." (857)

LV

    Mult fu lied et joius Carlemaines li ber,
    Ki tel rei ad cunquis sanz bataille campel.
860 Que vus en ai jo mes lunc plait a acunter? (860)
    Il passent les païs, les estrange regnez,
    Venuz sunt a Paris, a la bone citet,
    E vunt a Saint Denis, al muster sunt entrez;
    Karlemaines se culcet a oreisuns, li ber. (864)
865 Quant il ad Deu preiet, si s'en est relevet;
    Le clou et la corune si ad mis sur l'auter,
    E les altres reliques depart par sun regnet.
    Iloec fud la reïne, al pied li est caiee: (868)
    Sun mautalent li ad li reis tut perdunet,
870 Pur l'amur del sepulcre que il ad aüret.

---

    (851) que a joie
    (854) ma amistet et ma a.
    (855) menporterez en f.
    (857) carleun
    (860) plait a cunter
    (864) se culcget a
    (868) li est caiet

They embraced and commended each other to God.

LIV

    After the Frenchmen have eaten, they prepare to depart;
850 The mules and sumpters are kept ready by the horse-blocks; (850)
So the Frenchmen mount up, then depart, filled with joy.
King Hugo's daughter rushes up to them
Where she sees Oliver, she seizes him by the hem of his cloak:
"I have placed my affection and love in you;
855 Take me along to France; thus shall I go with you!"
"Fair Lady," said Oliver, "I give you my love as a gift:
I shall go back to France with Charles, my lord."

LV

    Charlemagne the Valiant was very happy and joyful
To have conquered such a king without a single pitched battle;
860 What more could I tell you?
They ride back through countries, foreign kingdoms;
They have reached Paris, the good city,
And they go to Saint-Denis; they have entered the church;
Charlemagne the Valiant prostrates himself on the ground in prayer.
865 After praying to God, he rose to his feet;
He put both the nail and the crown on the altar,
And distributed the other relics throughout his kingdom. (867)
The Queen was there; she has crouched at his feet:
The King has completely forgiven her spite,
870 For the sake of the Sepulchre that he has worshipped.

Notes to the Text and Translation

Except when otherwise noted, the references to Koschwitz are to his fourth edition, 1900; those to Aebischer are to his 1965 edition; the references to Favati and Tyssens are, respectively, to their 1965 edition and 1978 translation. The references to Horrent are to his 1961 analysis of the poem.

1. *fu karleun* (MS). Here (and also in lines 17, 112, 123, and 130) most modern scholars have emended *Karleun* to (*li*) *reis Charles*, in order to restore the meter. Aebischer corrected with *Carlemaine*, an emendation introduced by Koschwitz in his first edition (1879). However the Emperor's name appears only in line 166. See also note 158.

3. The pommel of a sword is the metal knob which terminates its hilt and balances the weapon.

8. *a reisuner* (MS). In the poem assonances are generally correct. But here and in a few other instances the usual distinction between assonances in -*e* and in -*ie* is not maintained. We agree with Horrent (p. 49, n. 1) that this may be a case of poetic license and, consequently, we have not corrected the endings involved (lines 63, 238, 305, 306, 308, 313, 314, 459, 541, 562, 589, 682, 778, 832, 868).

11. *espeez* (MS). There is a frequent confusion throughout the poem between final -*z* and final -*t*. We have decided not to correct these numerous cases.

17. *charle* (MS). See note 1.

43. *que ne se puet estorcer* (MS). We have adopted the correction *estordre* used by Koschwitz and Aebischer, which makes line 43 the first of the new *laisse*.

50. *barnez* (MS). It might mean here: "personal nobility, power" or "whole body of barons." (See Tyssens, p. 33).

63. *berenger* (MS). See note 8.

71. Thrice-repeated dreams are a common theme in the literatures of Antiquity and the Middle Ages. H. Braet (1975, pp. 42-43) suggested that the latter period was probably more influenced by the Biblical triple dreams of Joseph and Saint Peter.

74. The presence of camels among the pilgrims is rather surprising. These exotic animals are mentioned only here at the beginning of the poem. In the *Chanson de Roland*, seven hundred camels were part of numerous presents which were to be sent to Charlemagne by the Saracens (line 31). Martín de Riquer (1968, pp. 75-76) has emphasized that the Christians heard about camels after these animals had helped the Saracens defeat the men of Alfonso VI at the battle of Zalaca in 1086.

80. Here the poet lists some of the most typical attributes of the real pilgrim: the staff and the scrip, a small bag, or satchel. This picture is completed in lines 242-243: when the Franks reach Jericho, they cut palms, which makes them true palmers (*paumiers*), or pilgrims going to the Holy Land. Then they shout their traditional rallying cry: "Forward! So help us God."

81. *E funt ferrer les destres de tres et de uvant* (MS). The meter of this line is erroneous. It is clear that the Frenchmen are going on a pilgrimage and that they do not need war-horses (Horrent, p. 27, n. 3). Line 79 also points to the adopted emendation.

82. A sumpter is a pack animal, a beast of burden.

100-106. A number of critics have rearranged these lines because of alleged inconsistencies in the itinerary followed by Charlemagne (Koschwitz, Horrent, pp. 29-32, Tyssens, p. 36). As in most other French medieval *chansons de geste*, the poet uses here real and imaginary place-names without making any attempt at geographical accuracy. For this reason, and following Aebischer and Favati, we have kept the readings and the order given by the MS.

117. *ben seelee et close* (MS). For Favati and Tyssens this hemistich meant: "solidly built," while Horrent (p. 34, n. 2) understood: "forbidden to laymen."

121. The Twelve Peers were Charlemagne's chief warriors. Several *chansons de geste* record their various names, which always include Roland and Oliver. The *Chanson de Roland* gives this list: Roland, Oliver, Gérin, Gérier, Bérengier, Otton, Samson, Engelier, Ivon, Ivoire, Anséis, and Girard. In our poem, the Twelve Peers include some of the heroes of the cycle of the King, and some belonging to the cycle of William of Orange (See lines 61-65). See G. Favati, pp. 37-39.

125. A "Majesty" is a picture of God (or sometimes of the Virgin Mary) seated in glory, giving his benediction with his right hand, and holding an orb in the other.

142. *en albe la citet* (MS). This line has been corrected in different ways. Among the critics who have kept the reading *albe*, some understood it as meaning "dawn" (Horrent, p. 35, n. 3, for example), while others (Aebischer, Favati, Tyssens) understood, we think correctly, "alb," the vestment of white linen.

143. The cope is a liturgical vestment which retains the features of the hooded cloak from which it originates.

158. *Aies nun charles sur tuz reis curunez* (MS). The first hemistich is one syllable too short. The addition of *Maines*, first made by Koschwitz, is dictated by the context and by the use, for the first time in the poem, of the Emperor's full name in line 166. See note 1.

160. Horrent (pp. 39-45) stressed the part played by the relics given to Charlemagne. He reminded us that all those listed in the poem were real to the people of the twelfth century, and that the poet is not trying to poke fun at them, as Aebischer (1956, pp. 163-164) has contended. The poet also reinforces the widespread belief that Charlemagne had been a great collector and purveyor of relics. See line 867.

189. The shift (*chemise*) was a linen undergarment worn by both sexes. The female's model had long, tight sleeves, and it reached to the ground, while the male's came only to the knees.

199. The mark was a European unit of weight, varying from eight ounces to two-thirds of a pound, used for gold and silver.

205. See note 121.

209. *li language* (MS). Here this term refers to communities of people belonging to various nationalities. See R. Levy (1947), L. Spitzer (1938), and H. G. Koll (1958).

210. Damask is a silk fabric originally made in the city of Damascus, woven in different colors.

211. Costmary (*coste*) is a flavoring herb which was formerly used in medicine.

213. It has been noted that this threat, directed against those who are gathered around Saint Mary's church to sell their goods, is an echo of Jesus' anger at the money-changers in the Temple (H. Morf, 1884, p. 191; Horrent, p. 45, n. 5).

226-232. These lines end with two different types of assonances (226-228: -*i*; 229-232: -*ei*). Some critics corrected the assonances in -*i* of lines 226-228 to -*ei*, and joined both *laisses* (Koschwitz in his first edition, for example); others kept two short distinct *laisses*, with a lacuna after line 228 (Koschwitz in his later editions). It seems that very little, if anything, is missing after line 228. For this reason, we have adopted Aebischer's solution which distinguishes two short *laisses*, without indicating any lacuna after line 228. See Horrent, p. 48, n. 3.

230-232. This is a clear reference to the *Chanson de Roland*, particularly to the tragic slaughter of Charlemagne's rear guard in the Pyrenees.

242. See note 80.

260. *monteles* (MS). G. Paris (1880, p. 28) was the first to suggest that this could be a place-name: *Montelès*. Horrent (p. 50, n. 2) and Aebischer accepted this viewpoint, while Favati and Tyssens considered that the term means "hillocks." We have chosen the latter interpretation. -*Dabilant* (MS). These peaks have been identified (Horrent, p. 50, n. 2) with the Anti-Lebanon mountain range, between Lebanon and Syria.

261. *La roche del guitume* (MS). In spite of several suggestions, no satisfactory identification of this place-name has been given. See Horrent, p. 50, n. 2.

263. The "eagle" is an architectural term which refers to either the gable of a house, or to the pediment of a temple (*O.E.D.*, III, 3, c).

266. The viburnum forms an extensive genus of shrubs and small trees. The flowers of most species are white and come in clusters.

268-269. The use of furs like ermine, sable, marten and beaver was widespread among the nobility of Byzantium. Although furs had been used in Western Europe for a long time, it was at the beginning of the twelfth century that these very valuable items of dress became fashionable among the upper classes of the West, when contacts with Byzantium and the Moslem world began to develop. Soon fine furs became such a symbol of luxury and wealth that their display was denounced by Saint Bernard and others. Furs could be used for payments and gifts, just like gold or silver. According to the literature of the period, minstrels who had performed very well were often rewarded with fine furs or fur garments.

270. Chess was a very popular game among the nobility, and it is often mentioned in the literature of the time. Occasionally, as we can see in several *chansons de geste*, a game of chess would result in a violent confrontation between players (See P. Jonin, 1970, and L.-F. Flutre, 1968). The game of *tables*, a kind of backgammon, was also popular. The rules of these games and of other games are given in the *Libro de ajedrez y tablas* of Alfonso el Sabio.

271. One favorite pastime of the nobility was hunting, especially bird hunting with the help of hawks and falcons. The *De arte venandi cum avibus* of Frederick II of Sicily provides very valuable information on this sport.

272. Orphrey is a richly ornamented embroidery.

288. *Une caiere sus le tent dor suzpendant* (MS). The various suggestions offered until now to emend this line are unsatisfactory. The reading that we propose uses the words which are already in the line, limiting the correction to a prefix. The verbal form *sustent* is found in the poem in line 521. See our note in *Z.f.r.P.*

304. This description of Charlemagne conforms to the ideal physical features of the male in the Middle Ages. In addition to strong and muscular arms and a slim waist, he is often represented with curly blond hair. The feminine beauty is also often portrayed with curly blond hair, blue-gray eyes, a white face, and red lips. She is slender, with a long neck and small, firm breasts.

310. The form *Hugun* is written out when it is used in the oblique case (46, 283, 302, 471, 533, 559) and also when it is the subject (310, 323, 394, 397, 401, 419, 437, 444, 454). We have kept these forms in all instances, except in line 466, because of the meter. In two cases the form *Hugun* (subject) is used with a nasal bar on the last *u* (478, 483), and we have transcribed it *Hugue*, because it is subject and also because of the meter. The abbreviation *Hug'*, when subject, has been transcribed *Hugue*. Whenever this abbreviation is used as an oblique case, we have recorded it as *Hugun* (670, 682, 778, 785, 802), except in two instances when the meter requires the form *Hugue* (822, 852).

332. The walls of medieval chambers were often covered with hangings, both to decorate them and to help keep them warmer.

334. The *perron* was a block of stone which could be found near buildings to make it easier for knights and ladies to mount a horse. In line 439 of our poem, the term refers to an interior staircase.

337. The ermine fur (*pelisse*) could be worn over the *chemise*. The *bliaut* (a type of tunic) was the main outer garment. In very cold weather, a mantel was worn over all the other garments. See notes 189 and 268.

338. See note 270.

340. *Receurent les destrers* (MS). The emendation to *somiers* (sumpters) is prompted by the understanding and correction of line 81. This is the only case in the poem when war-horses (*destrers*) refer to the pilgrims' mounts. In his review of Favati's edition, Horrent (1969) points out that *chevaus*, used in line 418, refers only to sumpters (p. 171).

352-361. Here, and in lines 373-377, the poet describes in great detail the complex and smooth working of these marvelous automats. Such wonders did exist in the palaces of Constantinople where they had struck those who had visited this magnificent city. Many references to automata representing birds, animals, and humans are found in medieval literature (See E. Faral, 1913, pp. 328-335).

363. In Old French, negative constructions are often reinforced with terms suggesting something of very little value: a glove, a button, a shallot, etc.

373-377. See note 352.

384. *li orages et hidus costis* (MS). The hapax legomenon *costis* has given rise to a number of corrections and translations. We prefer Horrent's suggestion (p. 58, n. 1) to relate it to coast. At the beginning of the storm, in line 369, the wind is blowing in from the seaports.

402-403. See note 304.

406. *u adun la citet* (MS). Several places called *Dun* have been identified in France. We agree with Horrent (p. 60, n. 2) that the reading of the MS is correct, and that it is not necessary to replace *Dun* by *Verdun*, as proposed by A. Thomas (1903).

411. These fowls are often mentioned in the *chansons de geste* and seem to have been enjoyed at medieval banquets. Holmes (1952) commented that ". . . the cranes were served because they were captured with great sport by the hunting falcons and the mediaeval man liked to eat whatever he brought home from the hunt." (p. 89)

412. Clary (*claret*) was a popular sweet liquor made with wine, honey, and various spices.

413. Minstrels played an important role in medieval society. They were public entertainers carrying on popular traditions in different ways. Some of them were poets, but most were story tellers and singers using the works of others. Those who could play musical instruments often accompanied themselves on the *vielle*, a small oval fiddle with a box-soundchest and three strings. The *rote* was a kind of harp with five strings. See E. Faral (1910).

416. A *seneschal* was a trusted knight in charge of a large household. He was responsible for regulating and supervising all domestic arrangements.

418. *lur chevaus* (MS). See note 340.

423. The carbuncle was a large, brilliant stone which, in the Middle Ages, was said to have the property of emitting a powerful light in the dark. In the *Chanson de Roland*, we find this description of Baligant's navy: "At the mastheads and on the high prows/ There are many carbuncles and lanterns./ They cast such a glow from on high/ That the sea is made more beautiful through the night./ And when they reach the land of Spain,/ The entire countryside gleams and is illuminated by them" (Brault, 1978, vv. 2632-2637).

426. Sendal was a thin silken material used for luxurious garments.

439. See note 334.

447. *Franceis furent as cambres* (MS). We have kept the plural form *as cambres* used also in lines 631, 644 and 684, in spite of the singular in line 435. As Tyssens pointed out (p. 55), all the beds are in a single room, according to common medieval practice.

454. A knight bachelor was an apprentice knight, or one who was in the service of another knight.

456. The hauberk was a piece of armor which protected the torso, the shoulders, the upper arms, and the head of the knight. It was made of tightly meshed metal links, which could be double. In the twelfth century, the helm could be worn over the hood of the hauberk; it was attached to it, and tied under the chin with straps.

458. See note 3.

466. *Refols* (MS). This reading was rejected by Koschwitz and also by Tyssens (p. 58). Horrent would have preferred to keep it (p. 79, n. 2), and also Favati (p. 187). Greimas (1968, p. 545) lists this adjective, with an example taken from a twelfth century text. - *Hugun* (MS). See note 310.

471. An oliphant is an ivory horn.

475. A postern is a small back door or gate in the fortification wall of a castle.
480-481. See note 268.
536-537. See note 456.
575. See note 363.
581. The almandine is a violet variety of the ruby spinel. Gems were thought to have magic and sometimes healing properties. The popular medieval lapidaries listed and discussed the mythical miraculous attributes of numerous stones, many of them precious.
583-588. In this boasting, Aïmer plans to become invisible, thanks to the stones or to the fish skin of his hat, in order to play a nasty trick on King Hugo. See Koschwitz, pp. 80-81.
585. See note 412.
594. *pin antif* (MS). In his first edition, Koschwitz read *pui* (mountain) instead of *pin* (pine). This reading was rightfully rejected by recent critics, except by Tyssens (p. 63). See notes 760 and 780.
595-596. We agree with Aebischer's interpretation of this scene (p. 92), and we have translated accordingly. He believed that the three shields are thrown up in the air (*voler*). It appears to be a demonstration of skill quite similar to Turpin's feat with the apples (lines 500-501). Other critics have understood that Bertrand flies off with the help of the shields used as wings.
606. The ell is an old unit of length varying between 27 and 45 inches.
631. *mes cambres* (MS). See note 447.
635. The byrnie was a coat of mail very much like the hauberk (see note 456).
659. At least one line is missing between lines 659 and 660. This lacuna would have contained an answer from Charlemagne.
706. See note 332.
707. See note 304.
719. *De vus mes volentez aamplir ço ne quier aveir* (MS). We concur with Horrent's understanding and correction of this faulty line (p. 96, n. 3), and then slightly modified in a subsequent study (1966, pp. 572-573). The second hemistich, which is too long, has to be cleared of its negative construction. The context, particularly the princess's reaction expressed in the next line (720), does require this emendation. Aebischer has maintained the second hemistich with the negative construction in order to support his overall interpretation of Oliver's attitude towards the princess. It has led to the portrayal of what we think is a somewhat excessively chaste character. Tyssens has offered solutions which try to conciliate these two opposite viewpoints (pp. 70-72).
724. *ne quier altre aveir* (MS). We see in *altre* a feminine pronoun (*another one*), rather than a neuter one (*anything*). In spite of Oliver's behavior towards Hugo's daughter at the end of the poem, we believe that here Oliver makes this kind of comment without really committing himself to the extent of sacrificing his duty to the Emperor.
726. This line has engendered much scholarly debate. Basing his reasoning on the Scandinavian versions of the poem, Aebischer (1956) first suggested correcting the line in this manner: "That night, the Count did not kiss her more than a hundred times" (pp. 676-677). Then, in his review of Horrent's major study of the

poem published in 1961, Aebischer (1962) brought to light that line 726 had been underlined with dots in the manuscript of the British Museum. He came then to the conclusion that a collator who had "a better manuscript," which did not contain the controversial line, decided to delete it (p. 839). Horrent (1966) founded his counterdemonstration on an analysis of the French and foreign traditions of the poem, and he rejected the view that the original version did not contain line 726 (p. 575).

746. *neiles* (MS). We have adopted the suggestion put forward by Wathelet-Willem (quoted by Horrent, p. 101, n. 1), that *neile* should be related to *nasle*, attested in Old French under *naliere* (lace, aglet).

753. Based on a study of the first lines of each *laisse* of the poem, Favati (p. 86, n. 157) pointed out that line 753 is parallel to line 735, which begins a new *laisse*. He concluded that it should be placed at the beginning of *laisse* XLVII, and that *fenduz* should be corrected to *fend*. We have subscribed to his solution. Aebischer did not follow this path and kept line 753 at the end of the previous *laisse*.

760. *pin* (MS). This form was read *pui* by Koschwitz, and also, more recently, by Tyssens. This reading was prompted by the term *estache*, in the next line (761), which usually means *post, stake*. However, Greimas (1968) did give an example of *estache* meaning *tie, binding*, attested at the end of the thirteenth century (p. 265). See notes 594 and 780.

780. *Desur un pin antif* (MS). The few scholars who had the opportunity to examine and copy the sole manuscript of the poem, now lost, did read *pin* (pine) (also in lines 594, 760, 783) and not *pui* (mountain), which appears elsewhere in the text (lines 106, 260). Tyssens recognized that the notion of old (*antif*) and young mountains pertains to modern science; she has suggested the reading of *pui autif* (high); instead of *antif* (p. 78).

820. *Que preisat barnet* (MS). This hemistich is one syllable too short. We have introduced the pronoun *ele* (she) to correct the meter. Here as in line 50, *barnet* might also mean: "whole body of barons."

822. *La femme lu rei hug'* (MS). Here, exceptionally, we have transcribed *hug'* as *Hugue*, because of the requirements of the meter. See note 310.

835. See note 411.

837. See note 413.

850. See note 334.

852. *La fille lu rei hug'* (MS). Here also, exceptionally, we have transcribed *hug'* as *Hugue*, for the meter. See notes 822 and 310.

867. See note 160.

Index of Proper Names

Abilant (puis d') 260, *Anti-Lebanon mountain range. See notes*, 260.
AIMER 579, HAIMER 64, *son of Aymeri de Narbonne; one of Charlemagne's Twelve Peers.*
AIMERI 765, AMERI 739, *son of Hernaut de Beaulande; father of Guillaume d'Orange.*
ALIXANDRE 366, *Alexander the Great.*
AMIRAL 432, *Emir.*
Antioche 49, *Antioch, ancient city of Asia Minor.*
Arabie 199, *Arabia.*

Baivere 101, *Bavaria, a former kingdom of southern Germany.*
BERENGER 63, 540, *one of Charlemagne's Twelve Peers.*
BERNARD de Brusban 65, BERNARD 553, 764, 771, *son of Aymeri de Narbonne; one of Charlemagne's Twelve Peers.*
BERTRAM 65, 94, 327, 565, 591, *son of Bernard de Brusbant, nephew of William; one of Charlemagne's Twelve Peers.*
Brusban *v.* BERNARD.
Burgoine 100, *Burgundy, former duchy in east-central France.*

Capadoce 48, *Cappadocia, in Asia Minor; territory held by the Saracens.*
CARLE(S) . . . *v.* KARLES.
CARLEMAINE(S) . . . *v.* KARLEMAINES.
Cartres 654, *city of Chartres (Eure-et-Loir).*
CHARLE(S) *v.* KARLES.
CHRISTUS 676, *Christ.*
COSTANTIN 366, *Constantine, Emperor of Byzantium.*
Costuntinoble 47, Constantinoble 262, Costentinoble 816, *Constantinople, capital of King Hugo's kingdom.*
CRISANS de Rome 367, *Crescentius, a member of a powerful Roman family (See G. Paris, 1880, pp. 45-46).*
Croiz partie 104, *probably an imaginary place-name.*

Denemarche (dux de) 519, *Duke Ogier. v.* OGER.
Dun 406, *eight such place-names have been identified in France (See Tyssens, 1978, p. 53).*

ERNALZ 64, ERNALZ de Girunde 566, *son of Aymeri de Narbonne; one of Charlemagne's Twelve Peers.*
Espaine 230, *Spain.*
ESTEFNE 165, *Stephen, saint.*

France 66, 100, 151, 161 . . ., *the Kingdom of France;* - (emperere de) F. 58, 76, 233, *Charlemagne.* See Seint Denis.
FRANCEIS 23, 88, 223, 237 . . ., *Frenchmen.*

GERIN 63, 602, *one of Charlemagne's Twelve Peers (See Horrent, 1961, p. 22, n. 3).*
Girunde *v.* ERNALZ.
GOLIAS 424, *Goliath, the giant of the Bible.*
Grece 47, Grice 105, *Greece;* - (paile) grizain 294, *Greek (cloth of silk).*
GUILLAMES *v.* WILLEME d'Orenge.
Guitume (roche del) 261, *imaginary place-name in the Orient.*

HAIMER *v.* AIMER.
HUGUN le FORT 46, 302, 670, 692 . . ., H. li FORZ 310, 394, 397, 401 . . ., HUGUN 283, 323, 471, 533 . . ., HUGUE 466, 478, 483, 527 . . ., HUGUE li FORZ 764, 800, 838, 845, H. le FORT 692, *King of Constantinople, Emperor of the East.*
Hungerie 101, *Hungary.*

Jerico 242, *city of Jericho, in the Jordan Valley.*
Jerusalem 69, 108, 154, 308, Jersalem 204, *Jerusalem.*
JHESU 170, 790, JHESUS 187, 674 *Jesus-Christ.*
JUDEUS 129, 172 *Jews.*

KARLEMAINES 166, 182, 190, 203 . . ., KARLEMAINE 250, CARLEMAINES 300, 307, 396, 400 . . ., CARLEMAINE 419, 673, 736, 752 . . ., CARLEMAIGNES 365, CARLEMAIGNE 791, CHARLES MAINES 158, *King of France, Emperor of the West.*
KARLES 1, 123, 128, 228 . . ., KARLE 118, 130, 151, KARLUN 275, CARLUN 298, 333, 494, 838 . . ., CHARLES 5, 17, 342, CHARLE 30, 39, CARLE 41, 51, 303, CARLES 91, 112, 320, 392 . . ., *King of France, Emperor of the West.*

Lalice 103, *Laodicea, ancient city in Asia Minor.*
Latine (la) 208, *(the) Latin (referring to the church of Saint Mary in Jerusalem).*
LAZARE 164, *Lazarus, saint.*
Loheregne 101, *Lorraine, former duchy in north-eastern France.*

MARIE 187, 207, *the mother of Jesus.*
MASEÜZ 430, *name of a fairy.*

NAIMON 62, *one of Charlemagne's Twelve Peers.*

OGER de Denemarche 63, OGERS 518, *one of Charlemagne's Twelve Peers.*
OLIVER 61, 404, 484, 693 . . ., *one of Charlemagne's Twelve Peers; companion of Roland.*
Orenge *v.* WILLEME.

Paris 36, 654, 862, Parys 60, *capital of France.*
Paternostre *v.* Saincte.

PERE 181, 326, *St. Peter*.
PERSAUNZ 102, *the Saracens*.
Perse 48, *Persia, Saracen country*.

ROLLAND 61, 307, 469, 484, ROLLANT 232, 276, *Charlemagne's nephew; one of his Twelve Peers*.
Romanie 106, *the Byzantine Empire*.
Rome *v*. CRISANS.

Saincte Paternostre 114, *church of Holy Paternoster*.
SARAZINS 224, 227, *the Saracens*.
Seint Denis 1, *basilica, in the town of the same name*; - Seint Denis de France 86, Saint Denis 863, *small market-town near Paris*.
SIMEON 163, *Simon, saint.*

TURCS 102, *the Saracens*.
TURPIN 64, 87, 202, 828, *Archbishop of Rheims; one of Charlemagne's Twelve Peers*.

WILLEME d'Orenge 62, WILLEMES d'Orenge 326, 507, WILLEME 739, GUILLAMES 744, *son of Aymeri de Narbonne; one of Charlemagne's Twelve Peers*.

Select Bibliography

I) *Editions and Translations*

Aebischer, P., *Le Voyage de Charlemagne à Jérusalem et à Constantinople. Texte publié avec une introduction, des notes et un glossaire.* (Textes littéraires français, 115) Geneva: Droz, 1965.

Bacciarello, A., *Il Pellegrinaggio di Carlomagno; brani scelti de poema in antico francese e glossario.* Rome, 1911. (Fragmentary edition).

Cooper, A. J., *Le Pèlerinage de Charlemagne publié avec un glossaire.* Paris: A. Lahure, 1925. (After Koschwitz, with addition of a translation into modern French and an English glossary).

Draskovic, V. *Putovanje Karla Velikog u Jerusalim i Carigrad.* Belgrade: Univerzitet u Beogradu, 1965. (Critical edition with a translation into Serbian).

Favati, G., *Il "Voyage de Charlemagne." Edizione critica a cura di Guido Favati.* (Biblioteca degli Studi Mediolatini e Volgari, 4) Bologna: Libreria Antiquaria Palmaverde, 1965.

Koschwitz, E., *Karls des Grossen Reise nach Jerusalem und Constantinopel. Ein altfranzösisches Heldengedicht.* 1st edition, Heilbronn: Henninger, 1879; 4th ed., 1900; 7th ed., Leipzig: Reisland, 1923.

Lommatzsch, E., *Die Pilgerfahrt Karls des Grossen*, in *Kleinere Schriften zur romanischen Philologie.* Berlin: Akademie-Verlag, 1954, pp. 203-223. (Free translation into German).

Michel, F., *Charlemagne, An Anglo-Norman Poem of the Twelfth Century, now First Published with an Introduction and a Glossarial Index.* London: William Pickering, 1836.

Sherwood, M., *The Merry Pilgrimage.* New York: The MacMillan Company, 1927. (Partial translation into English).

Tyssens, M., *Le Voyage de Charlemagne à Jérusalem et à Constantinople. Traduction critique.* (Ktemata, 3) Gand: E. Story-Scientia, 1978.

Voretzsch, C., *Einführung in das Studium der altfranzösischen Sprache; zum Selbstunterricht für den Anfänger.* Halle: Niemeyer, 1901. (The 1951 and 1955 editions were prepared by G. Rohlfs).

An edition by A. Cavaliere, listed by M. Tyssens (1978, p. xi), has not yet been published.

II) *Studies and Reviews*

Adler, A., "The *Pèlerinage de Charlemagne* in New Light on Saint-Denis," *Speculum*, 22, 1947, pp. 550-561.

Aebischer, P., *Les Versions norroises du "Voyage de Charlemagne en Orient." Leurs sources.* (Bibliothèque de la Faculté de Philosophie et Lettres de l'Université de Liège-Fasc. CXL) Paris: Société d'Edition "Les Belles Lettres," 1956.

―――, "Le Gab d'Olivier," *Revue belge de Philologie et d'Histoire*, 34, 1956, pp. 659-679.

―――, "Sur quelques passages du *Voyage de Charlemagne à Jérusalem et à Constantinople*." A propos d'un livre récent," *Revue belge de Philologie et d'Histoire*, 40, 1962, pp. 815-843.

Bates, R. C., "*Le Pèlerinage de Charlemagne*: A Baroque Epic," in *Studies by Members of the French Department of Yale University*, New Haven, 1941, pp. 1-47.

Bédier, J., *Les Légendes épiques*. 3rd ed., Paris: Champion, 1929, vol. IV, pp. 141-156.

Caulkins, J. H., "Narrative Interventions. The Key to the *Jest* of the *Pèlerinage de Charlemagne*," in *Etudes de philologie romane et d'histoire littéraire offertes à Jules Horrent à l'occasion de son soixantième anniversaire*, eds. J.-M. D'Heur and N. Cherubini, Liège, 1980, pp. 47-55.

Cavaliere, A., "Per il testo critico del *Pèlerinage Charlemagne*," in *Studi in onore di Italo Siciliano*. Florence, 1966, vol. I, pp. 213-223.

Coulet, J., *Etudes sur l'ancien poème français du "Voyage de Charlemagne en Orient."* (Publications de la Société des Langues romanes, XIX) Montpellier, 1907.

Cromie, M., "Le Style formulaire dans le *Voyage de Charlemagne à Jérusalem et à Constantinople*," *Revue des langues romanes*, 77, 1967, pp. 31-54.

Crosland, J., *The Old French Epic*. Oxford, 1951, pp. 208-218.

Cross, T. P., "The Gabs," *Modern Philology*, 25, 1927-1928, pp. 349-354.

Davis, J. W., "*Le Pèlerinage de Charlemagne*" and "*King Arthur and King Cornwall*." *A Study in the Evolution of a Tale*. In Diss. Abstr., 35, 1974/75, 397 A. (Dissertation Indiana University, 1974. Pp. 422).

Deroy, J., "Respect du code de l'amour dans le Gab d'Olivier," in *Actes du VIe Congrès International de la Société Rencesvals pour l'étude des épopées romanes* (Aix-en-Provence, 29 août-4 septembre 1973). Aix-en-Provence: Impr. du Centre d'Aix, 1974, pp. 241-251.

Favati, G., *Il "Voyage de Charlemagne en Orient."* Bologna: Libreria Antiquaria Palmaverde, 1964.

Gänssle-Pfeuffer, C., "*Majestez* und *vertut* in der *Karlsreise* Zur Problematik und Deutung der Dichtung," *Zeitschrift für romanische Philologie*, 83, 1967, pp. 257-267.

Grigsby, J. L., "A Note on the Genre of the Voyage de Charlemagne," in *Essays in Early French Literature presented to Barbara M. Craig*, eds. N. J. Lacy and J. C. Nash, York, S.C.: French Literature Publications, 1982, pp. 1-8.

Hatcher, A. G., "Contributions to the *Pèlerinage de Charlemagne*," *Studies in Philology*, 44, 1947, pp. 4-25.

Heinermann, Th., "Zeit und Sinn der *Karlsreise*," *Zeitschrift für romanische Philologie*, 56, 1936, pp. 497-562.

Heisig, K., "Zur *Karlsreise*," *Archiv für das Studium der neueren Sprachen und Literaturen*, 162, 1932, pp. 122-123.

―――, "Ein phrygisch-skythisches Sagenmotiv in der *Karlsreise*," *Germanisch-romanische Monatsschrift*, 15, 1965, pp. 194-195.

Holmes, U. T., "The *Pèlerinage of Charlemagne* and William of Malmesbury," *Symposium*, 1, 1947, pp. 75-81.
Horrent, J., "Sur les sources épiques du *Pèlerinage de Charlemagne*," *Revue belge de Philologie et d'Histoire*, 38, 1960, pp. 750-764.
-------, *Le Pèlerinage de Charlemagne. Essai d'explication littéraire avec des notes de critique textuelle.* (Bibliothèque de la Faculté de Philosophie et Lettres de l'Université de Liège - Fasc. CLVIII) Paris: Société d'Edition "Les Belles Lettres," 1961.
-------, "Contribution à l'établissement du texte perdu du *Pèlerinage de Charlemagne*," in *Studi in onore di Italo Siciliano*. Florence, 1966, vol. I, pp. 557-579.
-------, "Pèlerinage de Charlemagne à Jérusalem et à Constantinople," *Le Moyen Age*, 73, 1967, pp. 489-494. (Review of Aebischer's, Draskovic's, and Favati's critical editions).
-------, "Du *Voyage de Charlemagne* selon l'édition de Guido Favati," *Cahiers de Civilisation Médiévale*, 12, 1969, pp. 165-171. (Review of Favati's edition).
-------, "La *Chanson du Pèlerinage de Charlemagne* et la réalité historique contemporaine," in *Mélanges de langue et de littérature du moyen âge et de la Renaissance, offerts à Jean Frappier par ses collègues, ses élèves et ses amis.* (Publications romanes et françaises, 112) Geneva: Droz, 1970, pp. 411-417.
Koschwitz, E., "Ueber das Alter und die Herkunft der *Chanson du Voyage de Charlemagne à Jérusalem et à Constantinople*," *Romanische Studien*, 2, 1875, pp. 1-60.
-------, *Ueberlieferung und Sprache der "Chanson du Voyage de Charlemagne à Jérusalem et à Constantinople." Eine kritische Untersuchung.* Heilbronn: Henninger, 1876.
Krappe, A. H., "Hugo von Byzanz, der Plügerkönig," *Zeitschrift für französische Sprache und Literatur*, 59, 1935, pp. 361-366.
Levy, R., "Sur le vers 384 du *Pèlerinage de Charlemagne*," *Romania*, 64, 1938, pp. 102-104.
-------, "The Term *language* in *Le Pèlerinage de Charlemagne*," *Modern Language Notes*, 62, 1947, pp. 125-127.
-------, "Une Réplique à propos de l'apax° costif," *Romania*, 70, 1948, pp. 95-97.
Loomis, L. H., "Observations on the *Pèlerinage Charlemagne*," *Modern Philology*, 25, 1927-1928, pp. 331-349.
Moland, L., *Origines littéraires de la France.* Paris, 1863, new ed., 1866, pp. 100-118.
Morf, H., "Etude sur la date, le caractère et l'origine de la *Chanson du Pèlerinage de Charlemagne*," *Romania*, 13, 1884, pp. 185-232.
Neuschäfer, H. J., "*Le Voyage de Charlemagne en Orient* als Parodie der Chanson de geste. Untersuchungen zur Epenparodie in Mittelalter," *Romanistisches Jahrbuch*, 10, 1959, pp. 78-102.
Nicholls, J. A., "The *Voyage de Charlemagne*, a Suggested Reading of Lines 100-108," *Australian Journal of French Studies*, 16, 1979, pp. 270-277.
Niles, J. D., "On the Logic of *Le Pèlerinage de Charlemagne*," *Neuphilologische Mitteilungen*, 81, 1980, pp. 208-216.

Owen, D. D. R., "*Voyage de Charlemagne* and *Chanson de Roland*," *Studi Francesi*, 11, 1967, pp. 468-472.

Panvini, Br., "Ancora sul *Pèlerinage Charlemagne*," *Siculorum Gymnasium*, 13, 1960, pp. 17-80.

Paris, G., *Histoire poètique de Charlemagne*. 1865; rpt. Paris, E. Bouillon, 1905, pp. 337-344.

-------, "La Chanson du Pèlerinage de Charlemagne," *Romania*, 9, 1880, pp. 1-50.

Paris, P., "Notice sur la chanson de geste intitulée: *Le Voyage de Charlemagne à Jérusalem et à Constantinople*," *Jahrbuch für romanische und englische Literatur*, 1, 1859, pp. 198-211.

Picherit, J.-L., "Sur le vers 288 du *Voyage de Charlemagne à Jérusalem et à Constantinople,*" *Zeitschrift für romanische Philologie*, 99, 1983, pp. 512-513.

Pinson, M., "Un nouvel essai d'explication: *Pèlerinage de Charlemagne*, vv. 100-108," *Romanische Forschungen*, 89, 1977, pp. 266-268.

Richard, J., "Sur un passage du *Pèlerinage de Charlemagne*: le marché de Jérusalem," *Revue belge de Philologie et d'Histoire*, 43, 1965, pp. 552-555.

Riquer, Martín de, *Les Chansons de geste françaises*, 2nd ed. transl. I. Cluzel. Paris: Nizet, 1968, pp. 194-207.

Rossman, V. R., "The *Voyage de Charlemagne*," in Rossman, Vladimir R., *Perspectives of Irony in Medieval French Literature*. (De proprietatibus litterarum, series maior, 35). The Hague: Mouton, 1975, pp. 71-78.

Rychner, J., *La Chanson de geste. Essai sur l'art épique des jongleurs*. (Société de publications romanes et françaises, 53) Geneva: Droz, 1955, 27-28, 37, 68, 75, 90, 105-106, 114-115.

Scheludko, D., "Zur Komposition der Karlsreise," *Zeitschrift für romanische Philologie*, 53, 1933, pp. 317-325.

Schlauch, M., "The Palace of Hugon de Constantinople," *Speculum*, 7, 1932, pp. 500-514.

Schürr, F., *Das altfranzösische Epos*. Munich: M. Hueber, 1926, pp. 160-169.

Spitzer, L., "*Lenguages* dans *Pèlerinage de Charlemagne*, v. 209," *Modern Language Notes*, 53, 1938, pp. 20-21, and 553.

-------, "Un apax anc. fr. expliqué par l'anglais?" *Romania*, 69, 1946-1947, pp. 388-389.

Steffens, G., "Zur *Karlsreise*," *Zeitschrift für romanische Philologie*, 30, 1906, pp. 280-294.

Sturm, S., "The Stature of Charlemagne in the *Pèlerinage*," *Studies in Philology*, 71, 1974, pp. 1-18.

Süpek, O., "Une Parodie royale du moyen âge," *Annales Universitatis Scientiarum Budapestinensis de Rolando Eötvös Nominatae, Sectio: Philologica moderna*, 8, 1977, pp. 3-25.

Thomas, A., "Sur un vers du *Pèlerinage de Charlemagne*," *Romania*, 32, 1903, pp. 442-444.

Toja, G., "Il gab d'Olivier in un antico cantare italiano," *Cultura neolatina*, 24, 1964, pp. 95-102.

Tyssens, M., "Encore les *neiles de paile* (*Karlsreise*, v. 746)," *Marche romane*, 26, 1976, pp. 19-30.

Vigneras, L. A., "L'Abbaye de Charroux et la légende du *Pèlerinage de Charlemagne*," *Romanic Review*, 32, 1941, pp. 121-128.

Walpole, R. N., "Charlemagne's Journey in the East. The French Translation of the Legend by Pierre de Beauvais," *Semitic and Oriental Studies* (University of California Publ. in Semitic Philology), 11, 1951, pp. 433-456.

-------, "The Pèlerinage de Charlemagne Poem, Legend and Problems" *Romance Philology*, 8, 1955, 173-186.

-------, "Humor and People in Twelfth-Century France," *Romance Philology*, 11, 1958, pp. 210-225. (See especially pp. 218-219).

-------, "*Le Pèlerinage de Charlemagne*: Jules Horrent and its *réalité cachée*," *Romance Philology*, 17, 1963, pp. 133-145. (Review of Horrent's *Le Pèlerinage de Charlemagne. Essai d'explication*. . .).

Webster, K. G. T., "Arthur and Charlemagne. Notes on the Ballad of King Arthur and King Cornwall and on the Pilgrimage of Charlemagne," *Englische Studien*, 36, 1906, pp. 337-369.

III) *Works of General Interest*

Bédier, J., *Les Légendes épiques*. 4 vols. Paris: Champion, 1908-1921.

Braet, H., *Le Songe dans la chanson de geste au XIIe siècle*, in *Romanica Gandensia*, 15, Gent: Rijksuniversiteit te Gent, 1975.

Brault, G. J., ed., *The Song of Roland. An Analytical Edition*. 2 vols. University Park/Pennsylvania and London: Pennsylvania State University Press, 1978.

Castets, M. F., ed., *Descriptio*. . . in *Revue des langues romanes*, 36, 1892, pp. 439-474.

Couraye du Parc, J., ed., *Mort Aymeri de Narbonne*. Paris: SATF, 1884.

Doutrepont, G., *Les Mises en prose des épopées et des romans chevaleresques du XIVe au XVIe siècle*. Brussels: 1939.

Faral, E., *Recherches sur les sources latines des contes et romans courtois du moyen âge*. Paris: Champion, 1913.

-------, *Les Jongleurs en France au moyen âge*. Paris: Champion, 1910.

Flutre, L.-F., "La Partie d'échecs de Dieudonné de Hongrie," in *Mélanges offerts à Rita Lejeune*. . ., 2 vols. ed. J. Duculot, Gembloux, 1968, pp. 757-768.

Greimas, A. J., *Dictionnaire de l'ancien français*. . . 2nd ed. Paris: Larousse, 1978.

Holmes, U. T. Jr., *Daily Living in the Twelfth Century*. Madison, Wisc.: The Univ. of Wisconsin Press, 1952.

Jonin, P., "La Partie d'échecs dans l'épopée médiévale," in *Mélanges de langue et de littérature du Moyen Age et de la Renaissance offerts à Jean Frappier*. . ., 2 vols., Geneva, 1970, pp. 483-497.

Koll, H.-G., *Die französischen Worter "langue" und "langage" im Mittelalter*. (Kölner romanistische Arbeiten, Heft 10) Geneva: Droz, 1958.

Levillain, L., "Essai sur les origines du Lendit," *Revue historique*, 152, 1927, pp. 241-276.

Paris, G., *Histoire poétique de Charlemagne*. 1865; rpt. Paris: E. Bouillon, 1905.

Roques, M., ed., *Aucassin et Nicolette, chantefable du XIIIe. siècle*. 2nd ed., Paris: Champion, 1973.

OHIO UNIVERSITY LIBRARY

Please return this book as soon as you have finished with it. In order to avoid a fine it must be returned by the latest date stamped below.

JAN 4 1988

NOV 3 1987

JUN 16 1995
QUARTER LOAN

MAY 25 1995

NOV 19 1985